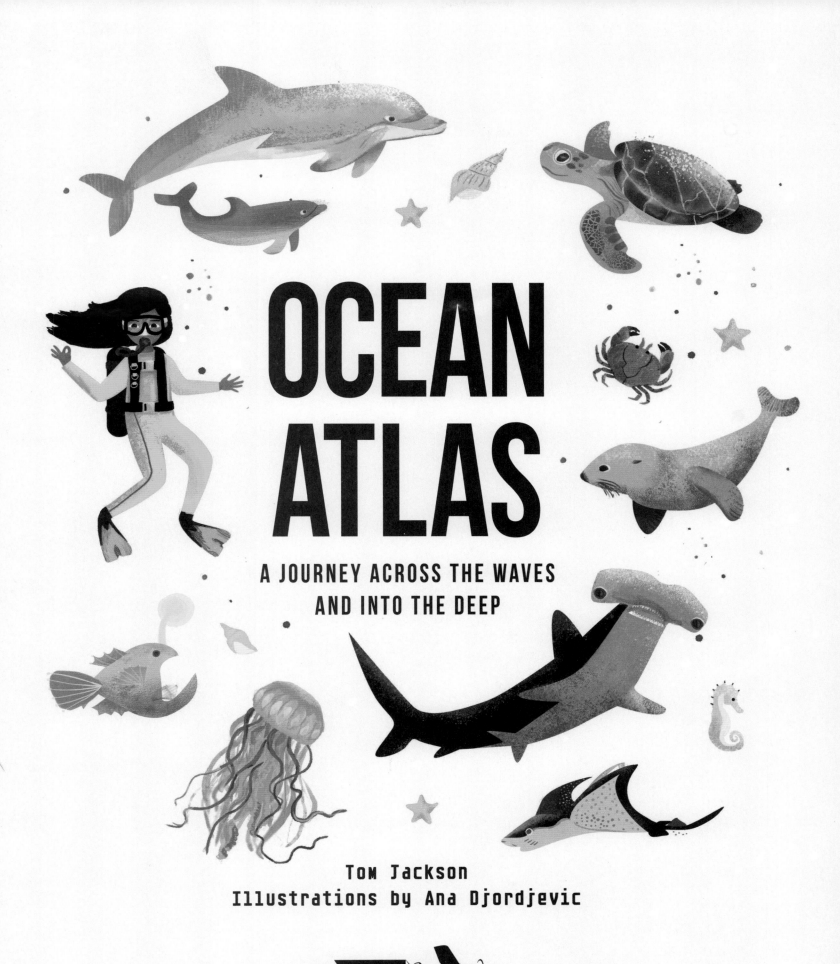

OCEAN ATLAS

A JOURNEY ACROSS THE WAVES AND INTO THE DEEP

Tom Jackson

Illustrations by Ana Djordjevic

QEB

Quarto is the authority on a wide range of topics.

Quarto educates, entertains and enriches the lives of our readers—enthusiasts and lovers of hands-on living.

www.quartoknows.com

Author: Tom Jackson
Illustrator: Ana Djordjevic
Editorial: Claire Throp & Emily Pither
Design: Sarah Andrews & Victoria Kimonidou

© 2020 Quarto Publishing plc

First Published in 2020 by QEB Publishing,
an imprint of The Quarto Group.
26391 Crown Valley Parkway,
Suite 220
Mission Viejo, CA 92691, USA
T: +1 949 380 7510
F: +1 949 380 7575
www.QuartoKnows.com

A CIP record for this book is available from the Library of Congress.

ISBN: 978-0-7112-5186-1

Manufactured in Guangzhou, China EB042020

9 8 7 6 5 4 3 2 1

PICTURE CREDITS

36l MARUM – Zentrum für Marine Umweltwissenschaften, Universität Bremen.

ALAMY: 26tr Norbert Wu/ Minden Pictures .

SHUTTERSTOCK: p4l Romolo Tavani, p7br Sergey Novikov, p11r Atypeek Dsgn, 12tr iurii, 15br BMJ, 16bl Anton Balazh, 19tr James Steidl, 20l Ethan Daniels, 22l Choksawatdikorn, 24bl nazz lopez, 28bl Mia Stendal, 31tr Ethan Daniels, 34br CHEN WS, 38r Mason Lake Photo, 40l Denis Burdin, 40r Sviluppo, 43br tryton2011, 44br Matt Berger, 49br Filippo Carlot, 50tr Deni_Sugandi, 52bl Harvepino, 53tr Everett Historical, 56r Ustyna Shevchuk, 58bl JC Photo, 60br Signature Message.

CONTENTS

Journey with me across the waves and into the darkest depths of the ocean. Take a deep breath and dive in!

INTRODUCTION

You live on what is known as a water planet. The dry land under your feet makes up little more than a quarter of the Earth's surface. The rest of the planet is covered by a thick layer of seawater. Let's take a journey through the world's oceans: we'll visit the weird seascapes at the bottom of the sea, go eye to eye with some spooky sea creatures, and even take a look inside a hurricane!

On a map, the world's seawater is divided into many sections. The biggest are the five oceans, but there are dozens of other smaller seas around the coasts. The names of our seas and oceans are useful for knowing where you are, if you are sailing across the sea or looking for an island or coastline. However, don't be fooled by them. You can see from the map on this page that all the water is joined together. Earth really has just one ocean: the World Ocean. The area it covers is 17 times as large as Russia, the world's largest country, and it contains enough water to fill 10 billion baths! In its deepest parts, it could easily swallow up Mount Everest and the rest of the Himalayas.

We measure the height, or altitude, of everything on land from sea level... so the surface of the ocean has an altitude of 0 feet.

Beaufort Sea

Labrador Sea

Gulf of Alaska

NORTH AMERICA

Sargasso Sea

North Atlantic Ocean

Caribbean Sea

SOUTH AMERICA

South Atlantic Ocean

OCEAN BASICS

The oceans fill enormous hollows in the Earth's surface that sit between large masses of land called continents. Far out from the coast, most of the ocean is about 2.2 miles (3.5 km) deep. The distance from seabed to surface is more than four times the height of Burj Khalifa, the world's tallest building.

2,717 feet (828 m)

The water in the oceans is very salty—far too salty to be safe to drink. The salt in seawater originally came from rocks, and over billions of years of rain it has washed into the oceans. When added to water, the white crystals dissolve, meaning they mix so well with the water that they disappear.

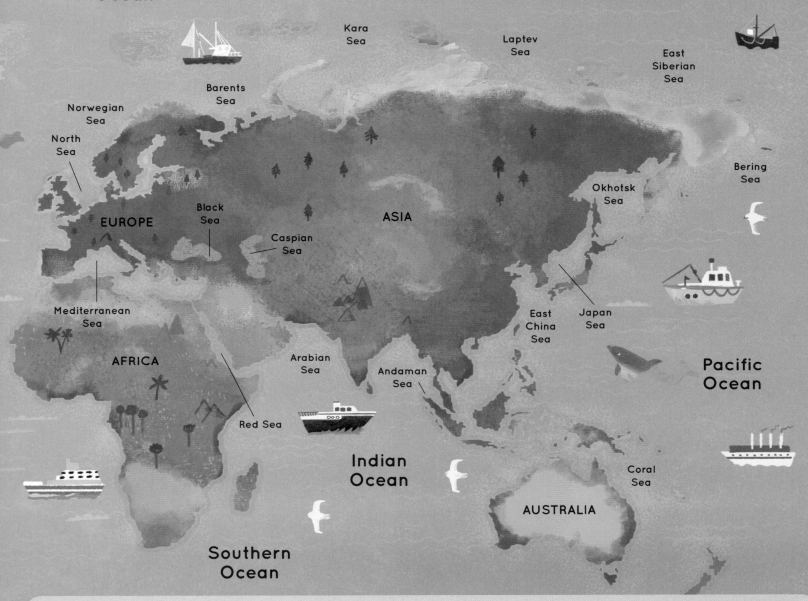

Arctic
Ocean

Kara
Sea

Laptev
Sea

East
Siberian
Sea

Barents
Sea

Norwegian
Sea

North
Sea

Bering
Sea

Black
Sea

Okhotsk
Sea

EUROPE

ASIA

Caspian
Sea

Mediterranean
Sea

East
China
Sea

Japan
Sea

AFRICA

Arabian
Sea

Andaman
Sea

Pacific
Ocean

Red Sea

Indian
Ocean

Coral
Sea

AUSTRALIA

Southern
Ocean

OCEANOGRAPHERS

Although the ocean covers so much of the planet, we still have lots to learn about it. The job of studying the seas belongs to scientists called oceanographers. They study waves, ocean currents, and the links between the weather and the seas. They are also trying to find out more about the sea floor. It is not easy to see down through all that water, and we have better maps of the Moon and Mars than we do of our own seabed! What will we find next down there in the deep?

THE ATLANTIC OCEAN

The Atlantic Ocean is the second largest ocean on the Earth. It runs between North and South America to the west, and Europe and Africa to the east. The ocean got its name from the myth of Atlantis, which tells the story of a great city disappearing below the ocean in a terrible flood. Ancient writers disagreed where the city of Atlantis was, but Plato, a famous Greek philosopher, said the lost city lay beneath the sea, far to the west of Africa. As such, this area of ocean became known as the Atlantic.

· ·

AREA: 41,104,500 square m (106,460,000 sq km)

VOLUME: 23% of World Ocean

COAST LENGTH: 69,510 m (111,866 km)

WIDEST POINT: 3,977 m (6,400 km) Argentina to South Africa

NARROWEST POINT: 1,770 m (2,848 km) Brazil to Sierra Leone

AVERAGE DEPTH: 11,962 ft (3,646 m)

DEEPEST POINT: Milwaukee Deep (near Puerto Rico), 27,841 ft (8,486 m)

MAIN ISLANDS: Iceland, Great Britain, Ireland, Cuba, Hispaniola

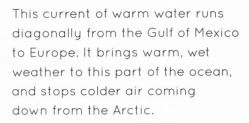

This current of warm water runs diagonally from the Gulf of Mexico to Europe. It brings warm, wet weather to this part of the ocean, and stops colder air coming down from the Arctic.

NORTH AMERICA

CHRISTOPHER COLUMBUS

· ·

Until the 15th century, European sailors believed that China, India, and the mysterious Spice Island (now known as Indonesia) lay on the far side of the Atlantic Ocean. It was so far that it would take months to sail across, and no crew would survive using the ships of the time. However, in 1492 Christopher Columbus thought the world was much smaller than this and said he could sail all the way to Asia in three weeks. After four weeks at sea, the ships arrived at land, only it was America, not Asia, that they discovered.

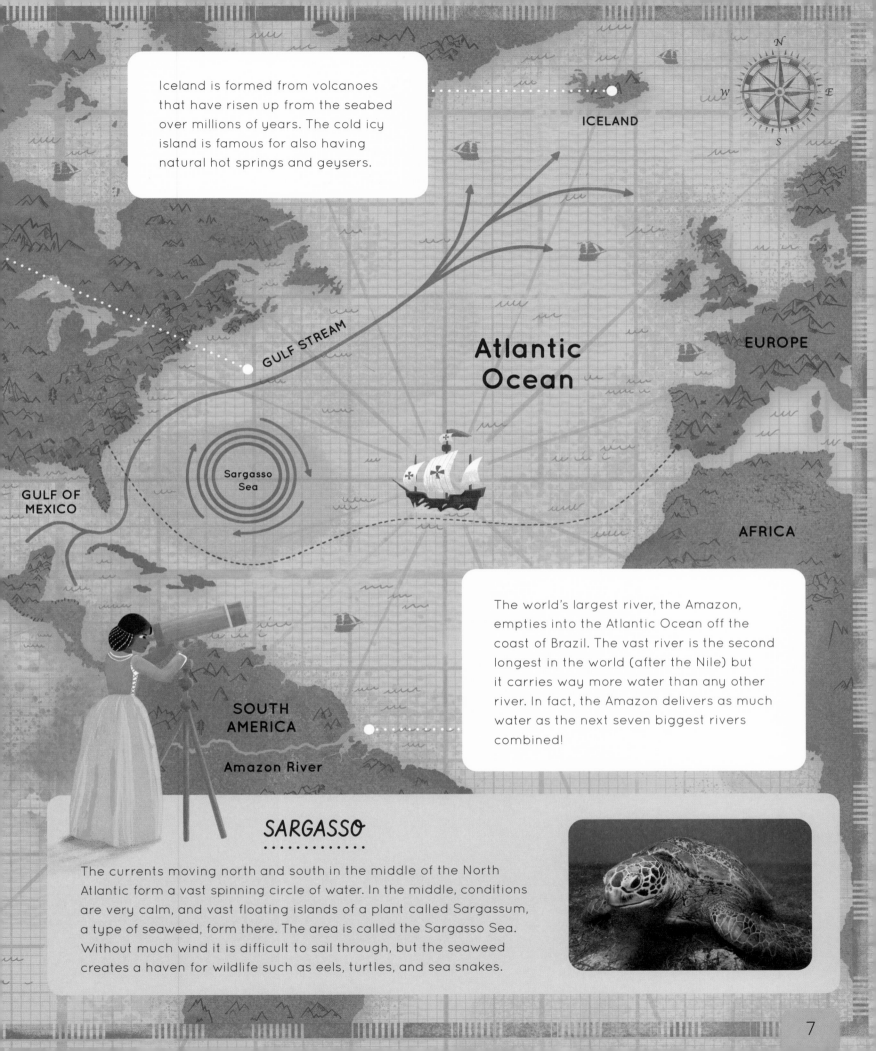

Iceland is formed from volcanoes that have risen up from the seabed over millions of years. The cold icy island is famous for also having natural hot springs and geysers.

ICELAND

GULF STREAM

Atlantic Ocean

EUROPE

GULF OF MEXICO

Sargasso Sea

AFRICA

The world's largest river, the Amazon, empties into the Atlantic Ocean off the coast of Brazil. The vast river is the second longest in the world (after the Nile) but it carries way more water than any other river. In fact, the Amazon delivers as much water as the next seven biggest rivers combined!

SOUTH AMERICA

Amazon River

SARGASSO

The currents moving north and south in the middle of the North Atlantic form a vast spinning circle of water. In the middle, conditions are very calm, and vast floating islands of a plant called Sargassum, a type of seaweed, form there. The area is called the Sargasso Sea. Without much wind it is difficult to sail through, but the seaweed creates a haven for wildlife such as eels, turtles, and sea snakes.

THE PACIFIC OCEAN

The Pacific Ocean covers more of the surface of Earth than all the dry land added together. Its area is almost as big as the total area of all the other oceans put together, and it has about half of all the world's seawater. This ocean is surrounded by four of the seven continents. About 20,000 years ago the Bering Strait, which links the Pacific to the Arctic Ocean, was closed by dry land. That formed a bridge for people to make their way into the Americas for the first time. And 2,000 years ago, adventurous explorers sailed from island to island in search of new homes, until they had spread right across the Pacific. The last place to be settled was New Zealand, about 800 years ago.

AREA: 63,800,000 square m (165,250,000 sq km)

VOLUME: 49% of World Ocean

COAST LENGTH: 84,297 ms (135,663 km)

WIDEST POINT: 12,000 m (19,300 km), Colombia to Malaysia

NARROWEST POINT: 620 m (1,000 km), Drake Passage, from Tierra del Fuego to Antarctica.

AVERAGE DEPTH: 14,042 ft (4,280 m)

DEEPEST POINT: 36,070 ft (10,994 m), Challenger Deep (near Guam)

MAIN ISLANDS: New Guinea, Japan, New Zealand, Hawaii

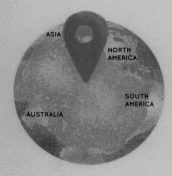

MARIANA TRENCH

The deepest point on Earth—Challenger Deep—is under the Pacific Ocean at the bottom of a vast crack in the seabed called the Mariana Trench. It is 36,070 feet (10,994 m) below the surface. Mount Everest is 29,029 feet (8,848 m) high, so if we lowered it into the trench, there would still be more than 1.2 miles (2 km) of water above its summit.

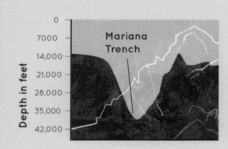

MARIANA TRENCH

RING OF FIRE

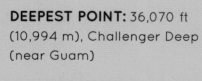

Around the Pacific Ocean's coast are 452 volcanoes. That is more than three-quarters of all active volcanoes in the world. Together, the volcanoes are called the Pacific Ring of Fire.

INTERNATIONAL DATE LINE

THE PEACEFUL OCEAN

The name Pacific means peaceful. It was the Portuguese explorer Ferdinand Magellan who came up with the name as he led the first voyage to sail all the way around the world. In 1520, Magellan led his fleet through the stormy seas around the bottom of South America to reach a vast, calm ocean. Magellan declared it was Mar Pacifico, or "Peaceful Sea." However, once the adventurers had sailed across the ocean, they got caught up in a local war in the Philippines and Magellan was killed!

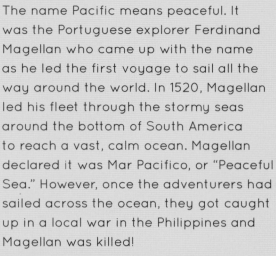

The International Date Line (IDL) is an imaginary line running down the middle of the Pacific. Something strange happens there. Imagine you are on a ship just west of the line; it is midday on January 1. When your ship sails east of the IDL, the time is still 12 pm but the date is now December 31. You have moved back in time!

Pacific Ocean

Galapagos Iguana

GALAPAGOS ISLANDS

Giant Tortoise

Galapagos Penguin

Formed from the lava left behind by undersea volcanoes, the Galapagos Islands are home to some unusual animals, including iguanas and penguins that live 5,600 miles (9,000 km) from Antarctica. However, the most famous residents are the giant tortoises, which grow as long as a bed, weigh as much as a horse, and live for more than 100 years.

THE INDIAN OCEAN

The name Indian Ocean dates back to the days of ancient Rome. In those days, geographers did not really know what lay to the east of their empire. They had heard of a mighty river there called the Indus, and they named the whole region around it India. (The local name for the river is the Sindhu, and today most of it is actually in Pakistan, not India.) So this eastern sea was marked on ancient maps as the Indian Ocean. However, the name hides the fact that this ocean—the third largest—connects Africa to India, China, Southeast Asia, and Australia. It is thought that the first oceangoing humans sailed up and down the coast of the Indian Ocean in simple boats, and moved from Africa to southern Asia 70,000 years ago. They reached Australia more than 50,000 years ago.

· ·

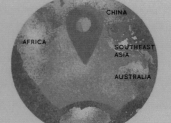

AREA: 28,355,000 square m (73,440,000 sq km)

VOLUME: 20% of World Ocean

COAST LENGTH: 41,337 ms (66,526 km)

WIDEST POINT: 4,720 m (7,600 km), from Africa to Australia

AVERAGE DEPTH: 12,274 ft (3,741 m)

DEEPEST POINT: 23,812 ft (7,258 m), Java Trench (near Indonesia)

MAIN ISLANDS: Madagascar, Sri Lanka, Indonesia

Until 1869, a voyage between Asia and Europe meant sailing all the way around Africa. The Suez Canal changed that by connecting the Red Sea—part of the Indian Ocean—to the Mediterranean Sea. The canal is 120 miles (193 km) long and about 17,200 ships a year take this shortcut.

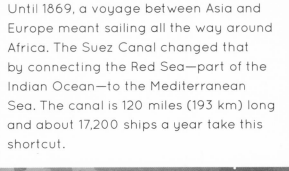

Mediterranean Sea

Suez Canal

Red Sea

SAUDI ARABIA

Arabian Sea

AFRICA

Cape Agulhas

The Indian Ocean and the Atlantic Ocean meet at Cape Agulhas, the southernmost tip of Africa. The sea around the cape is famous for powerful storms and huge waves that surge up suddenly to heights of 100 feet (30 m).

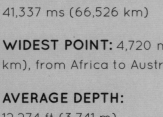

In the 1500s, European explorers sailed to the islands of Southeast Asia. They knew these lands as the Spice Islands because many exotic spices, such as nutmeg and cloves, came from there. The spices were used to flavor food and were traded via a long overland route through Asia, controlled by powerful merchants.

Cinnamon

Nutmeg

Cloves

COELACANTH

Deep in the Indian Ocean lives a rare and unusual fish called the coelacanth (pronounced "see lah kanth"). It is about 6.5 feet (2 m) long and weighs 176 pounds (80 kg)—about the same as a big man. The coelacanth lives among the rocks of the deep ocean floor, and spends the days in underwater caves. It can swim but also gets around on the seafloor using its sturdy fins. The coelacanth's fins are made of thick bone—similar to our arms and legs. In fact, the coelacanth is the last surviving relative of the fish that evolved (around 350 million years ago) into today's land animals—including mammals like us!

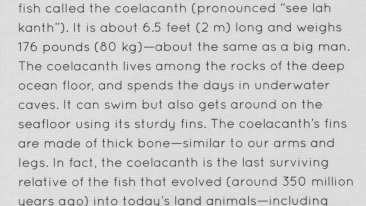

INDIA

Indian Ocean

AUSTRALIA

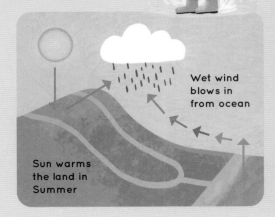

MONSOON

The Indian Ocean is famous for its monsoon, which is a time of year when the wind blowing in from the sea brings heavy rain to the land that surrounds the ocean, most famously in southern Asia. The monsoon provides water for crops and rivers, but can also create dangerous flooding. The monsoon appears in summer when the land is warmer than the ocean. This difference makes the winds change direction and blow toward the land. In winter, the land cools down, and the winds change again, making everything much drier on land.

Wet wind blows in from ocean

Sun warms the land in Summer

THE ARCTIC OCEAN

Located at the top of the globe, it sometimes takes a while to find the Arctic Ocean on a map. This is because the ocean water is often frozen, so it looks like an area of icy land. The Arctic Ocean is bordered by an imaginary line in the sea called the Arctic Circle. In winter the ocean is almost completely covered in a sheet of ice. About half of that melts away throughout the summer and starts to freeze again as autumn arrives. Ice that does not melt in summer gets thicker the next winter, and this can grow to many feet thick, especially where it gets squashed by more ice forming all around. Watching how the Arctic's ice is melting and freezing is a good way of understanding how global warming will affect the rest of the planet through climate change.

AREA: 5,427 square m (14,056 sq km)

VOLUME: 1.5% of World Ocean

COAST LENGTH: 28,203 m (45,389 km)

WIDEST POINT: 2,628 m (4,230 km)

NARROWEST POINT: 15 m (24 km), Kennedy Channel

AVERAGE DEPTH: 3,953 ft (1,205 m)

DEEPEST POINT: 17,877 ft (5,449 m), Litke Deep

MAIN ISLANDS: Greenland, Svalbard, Ellesmere Island, Novaya Zemlya

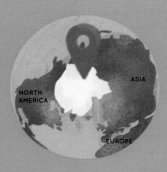

ICEBREAKER

It is possible to walk, ski, sled—and even drive—across parts of the Arctic Ocean, but the only way to explore all the ocean is by using an icebreaker. This is a very heavy ship with a thick hull and powerful engines that can smash through the ice. The bow of the ship is shaped so that it will slide up on top of the ice, and the great weight of the ship makes the ice crack beneath it.

The Arctic Ocean has two North Poles. The first is the Geographic North Pole, which is the most northerly point on the planet. This pole is the point around which the planet is spinning on its axis. The second pole is Magnetic North. This is the point where compasses point, and at the moment it is about 310 miles (500 km) from true north under Ellesmere Island.

Greenland is the world's largest island. It was discovered by the Vikings around 1,000 years ago, when the weather there was much warmer than it is now, so it really would have been a "green land."

The Arctic Ocean is home to the polar bear, the world's largest land carnivore. The polar bear can swim for many miles through water; it has wide feet that work well as paddles. However, the bear is most at home on the ice where it sniffs out seals and smashes through the ice to get them. The bear's skin is black, and the white fur is actually transparent, but it looks white from far away as it reflects the light. The hairs are hollow in order to trap warm air, which helps to keep the bear warm.

THE SOUTHERN OCEAN

The Southern Ocean is a bit different from the other four. Some people think it doesn't really exist! The other oceans take up an obvious region of Earth: their seabeds form a natural hollow in the surface and they are generally surrounded on most sides by land. The Southern Ocean only has land in the middle. It forms a ring of water around Antarctica, the ice continent at the southern end of the planet. The waters of the Southern Ocean extend to a latitude of 60° South. (Latitude is a way of measuring a position on Earth north or south from the Equator.) The limit of the Southern Ocean is set here because this is where the cold water from the Antarctic mixes with the warmer water in the Atlantic, Pacific, and Indian oceans.

AREA: 7,848 square m (20,327 sq km)

VOLUME: 5.5% of World Ocean

COAST LENGTH: 11,165 m (17,968 km)

AVERAGE DEPTH: 10,728 ft (3,270 m)

DEEPEST POINT: 23,737 ft (7,235 m), South Sandwich Trench

MAIN ISLANDS: South Shetland Islands, South Orkney Islands, Berkner Island, Alexander Island

There are about 1,350 islands in the Southern Ocean. Most of them are small icy rocks, but the largest, Alexander Island, is more than twice as big as Wales.

MIDNIGHT SUN

The Midnight Sun is caused by the way that Earth's axis is tilted. This tilt means that during December, the southern hemisphere is leaning toward the Sun. As Earth rotates, the southern hemisphere stays in the Sun for longer. The dark night side of Earth is covering more of the northern hemisphere. The days are long in the south, and this is what brings the warm summer conditions. None of the land south of the Antarctic Circle is on the night side of Earth. The sun stays up all day and night—even at midnight. Going farther south, this "midnight sun" stays up for days on end, and at the South Pole itself, the sun stays up for six months at a time. It then stays down for the following six months.

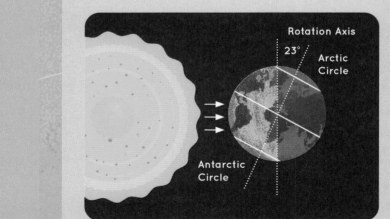

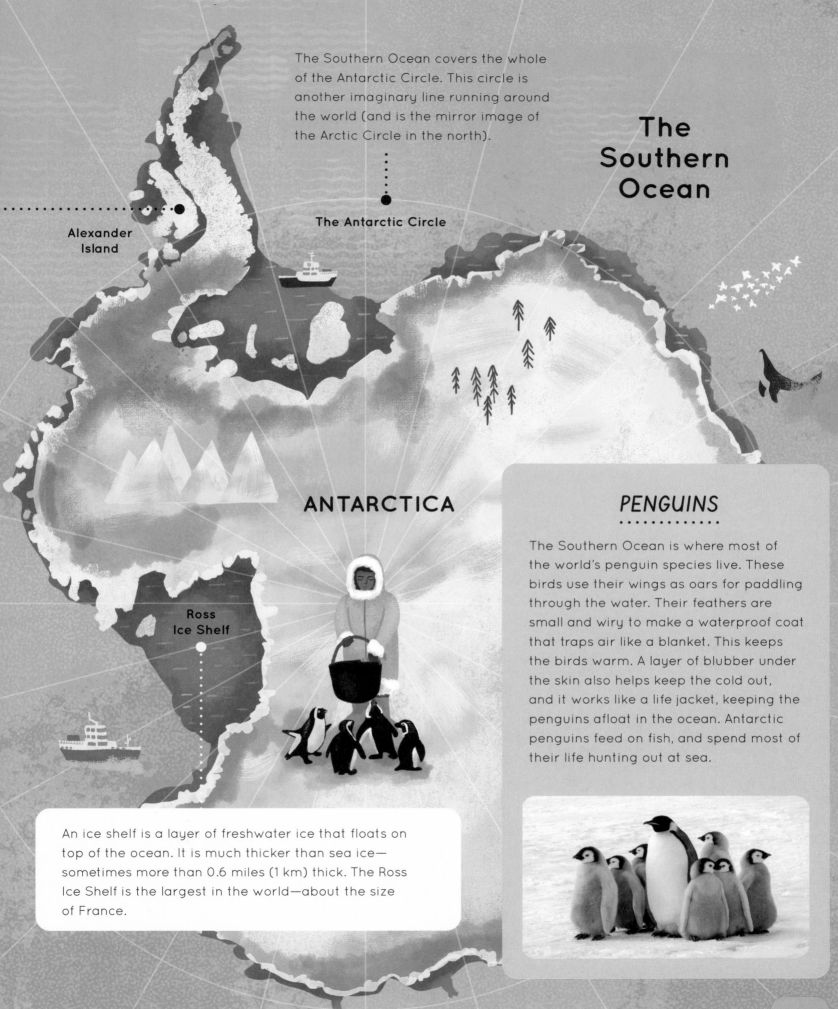

The Southern Ocean covers the whole of the Antarctic Circle. This circle is another imaginary line running around the world (and is the mirror image of the Arctic Circle in the north).

The Southern Ocean

Alexander Island

The Antarctic Circle

ANTARCTICA

Ross Ice Shelf

PENGUINS

The Southern Ocean is where most of the world's penguin species live. These birds use their wings as oars for paddling through the water. Their feathers are small and wiry to make a waterproof coat that traps air like a blanket. This keeps the birds warm. A layer of blubber under the skin also helps keep the cold out, and it works like a life jacket, keeping the penguins afloat in the ocean. Antarctic penguins feed on fish, and spend most of their life hunting out at sea.

An ice shelf is a layer of freshwater ice that floats on top of the ocean. It is much thicker than sea ice—sometimes more than 0.6 miles (1 km) thick. The Ross Ice Shelf is the largest in the world—about the size of France.

THE SEAS

Have you ever dreamed of sailing the Seven Seas? Well, you'd better update your route! The Seven Seas is an idea that comes from ancient times, before humans made detailed maps of the oceans. There are now at least 200 seas named around the world, although sailors and mapmakers have not agreed on an exact list. In general, any patch of ocean that is enclosed by land or islands is called a sea. Let's visit a few.

CASPIAN SEA

The oceans are fed by rivers, but sometimes rivers cannot reach the sea, and instead empty into lakes. The Caspian Sea—fed by Russia's Volga River—is a lake so large that we call it a sea, although it is 310 miles (500 km) inland from the nearest shore. The water slowly evaporates, leaving behind any dissolved minerals it contained. These minerals—mostly salt—build up so the Caspian's water is slightly salty, not fresh. Strangely, the Caspian is below sea level. The surface is 92 feet (28 m) lower than the surface of the World Ocean.

BEAUFORT SEA

☐ 68,725 square miles

■ 5,280 cubic miles

≡ 415,364 feet, Canada Basin

≋ Arctic

CARIBBEAN SEA

☐ 1,063,000 square miles

■ 1,454,000,000 cubic miles

≡ 25,217 feet, Cayman Trough, between Cuba and Jamaica

≋ Atlantic

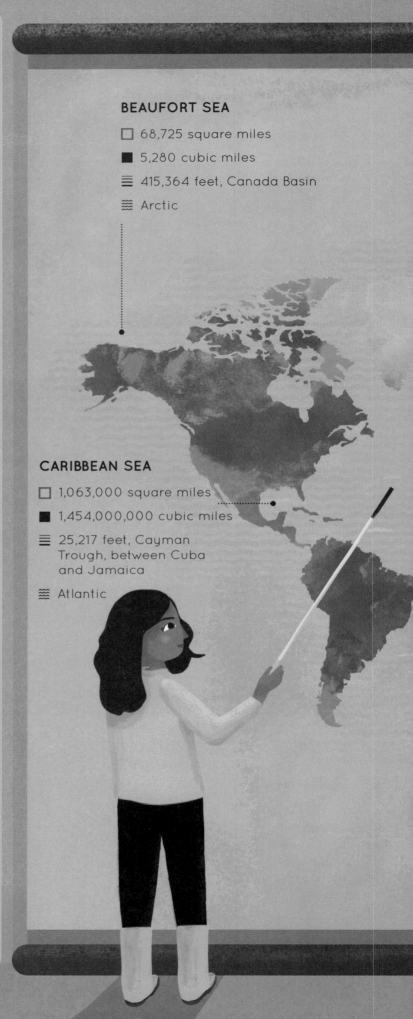

NORTH SEA

- ☐ 220,000 square miles
- ■ 12,955 cubic miles
- ≣ 2,300 feet, Norwegian Trench
- ≋ Atlantic

BALTIC SEA

- ☐ 146,000 square miles
- ■ 5,200 cubic miles
- ≣ 1,506 feet, on Swedish side
- ≋ Atlantic

BLACK SEA

- ☐ 168,000 square miles
- ■ 131,200 cubic miles
- ≣ 7,257 feet, near Turkish Coast

CASPIAN SEA

- ☐ 143,000 square miles
- ■ 18,760 cubic miles
- ≣ 3,363 feet

SOUTH CHINA SEA

- ☐ 1,351,000 square miles
- ■ 3,611,000,000 cubic miles
- ≣ 16,457 feet
- ≋ Pacific

RED SEA

- ☐ 169,000 square miles
- ■ 55,900 cubic miles
- ≣ 9,974 feet, Suakin Trough
- ≋ Indian

BAY OF BENGAL

- ☐ 839,000 square miles
- ■ 1,355,000,000 cubic miles
- ≣ 15,400 feet
- ≋ Indian

CORAL SEA

- ☐ 1,850,000 square miles
- ■ 2,752,000 cubic miles
- ≣ 29,987 feet
- ≋ Pacific

MEDITERRANEAN SEA

- ☐ 965,000 square miles
- ■ 900,000 cubic miles
- ≣ 17,280 feet, Calypso Deep, near Greece
- ≋ Atlantic

KEY ☐ Area ■ Volume ≣ Max Depth ≋ Ocean

EXPLORING THE DEPTHS

Now we know our way around the map of the oceans and seas, it's time to dive in and take a look at what is happening under the sea. Exploring the deep ocean will require some special technology. The oldest surviving watercraft are very simple boats, made by digging out the middle of a tree trunk to make a canoe. Some of these date back 10,000 years, but it is likely that our ancestors were using them many millennia before that. However, we have only really learned how to sail under the water in the last century or so.

HOW TO DIVE

A submarine floats because it has tanks filled with air. To dive beneath the surface, the air is released from these tanks, and water is allowed to take its place. The sub gets heavier and it sinks underwater. To surface again, air is pumped into the tanks, forcing the water out and making the sub rise. The air used for this is compressed (squashed) inside storage tanks so that it takes up very little space. Before it dives again, the submarine must refill its compressed air tanks or it will not be able to resurface.

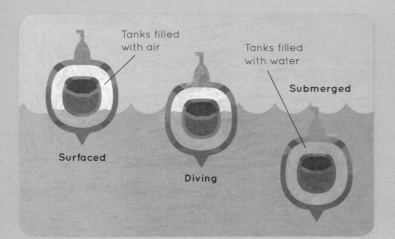

Tanks filled with air

Tanks filled with water

Submerged

Surfaced

Diving

Standing for Self-Contained Underwater Breathing Apparatus, scuba gear includes a tank of air, a mask over the face, and a mouthpiece (called a regulator). This allows divers to breathe in air from the tank, but blow it out into the water. Most divers can go to a maximum depth of about 130 feet (40 m).

Scuba

To go to the seabed, we need to use a bathyscaphe. This vessel is designed only to sink down in a straight line and then come back up again. The crew are inside a tiny cabin, and there are weights (for going down) and a float (for coming back up). Once on the seabed, the crew drops the weights, and the float takes over.

Bathyscaphe

DIVING BELL

This simple diving craft has no engine or moving parts. Air is trapped inside the bell and is held there by the water below pushing upward. The divers can swim out of the bottom, breathing through a pipe connected to the bell.

Submarine

A submarine can travel along the surface or dive underwater. Most submarines cannot go below a depth of about 330 feet (100 m) before the water pressure starts to bend the hull so much it cracks open—and makes the sub sink. Modern submarines are able to stay underwater for long periods. They can make drinking water from seawater, and recycle the air inside so it stays full of oxygen.

USS NAUTILUS

This US naval submarine was the first to be powered by a nuclear reactor. It did not need to be refueled and could go to sea for months on end—and stay underwater for all that time. In 1958, the Nautilus made a very unusual voyage. It sailed to the North Pole by diving under the ice.

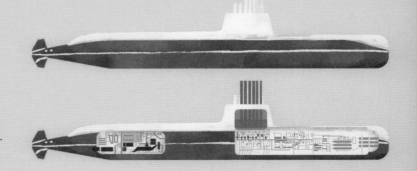

TIDAL ZONE

This is where the ocean meets the land. The water is always on the move due to the tides: the water rises up the shore to a high water mark, and then sinks back down to a low water level. There is one tide every 12 hours. Living in a place where water is constantly flooding in and then draining away makes the tidal zone half land and half ocean. The plants and animals that live in this area have to be able to survive in air and in water. Most tidal life shuts down when the tide goes out and waits for the water to return. Each plant or animal is built to survive out of the water for a different amount of time, so tidal wildlife forms into bands across the shoreline. Next time you are at the beach, take a look for yourself.

TIDAL RANGE

The tidal range, or distance between low and high tide, is normally between 6.5 and 10 feet (2-3 m). However, in places where the coastline forms a funnel shape, the tide surges a great distance up the shore. The largest tidal range of all is 53.5 feet (16.3 m) at the Bay of Fundy in Canada.

HOW DO TIDES WORK?

The tide is caused by the gravity of the Moon pulling on the ocean. When the Moon is overhead, its gravity creates a slight bulge in the surface of the ocean. As Earth rotates, the Moon hauls that bulge around the planet. Out at sea the tidal bulge is only 24 inches (60 cm) high, but when it hits land, the water rises up the shore creating a high tide. Earth continues rotating, and six hours later the water has sunk down to a low tide. A second bulge also forms on the far side of the world, which is why there is a high tide every time Earth makes half a turn, or every 12 hours. Every two weeks, the Sun's gravity aligns with the Moon's to make a spring tide, where the water rises extra high. In between there are weaker, or neap, tides.

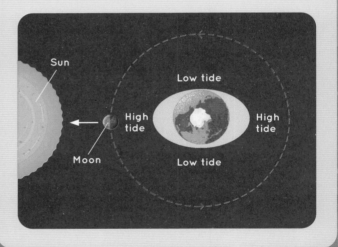

Low water

On the highest part of the shore, the only moisture comes from the spray of waves crashing against the coast. Barnacles live here, sifting food from the trickles of water, and closing up their shells to stay moist inside during drier times.

When the tide goes out, water—and sea life—is trapped in rock pools. These ponds will be refilled when the tide floods in again. As soon as the tide goes out, the rock pool's water starts to change. It gets saltier as water evaporates in the sunlight, and it also gets warmer.

Spray zone

High water

Mid water

In this zone, the water only covers the shore during high water, and maybe not at all during a neap tide. Seaweeds are small, tough, and leathery. The shellfish, such as winkles and limpets, firmly fix themselves onto rocks to hold water under their shells for long periods.

This zone is covered in water and then exposed to the air with every passing tide. The wildlife here is under the water for about the same amount of time as it is in the air. The seaweeds are covered in slime to stay damp in the air, and sea anemones curl up their tentacles into soggy blobs when the tide goes out.

The bottom of the shoreline is normally underwater, so it has large seaweeds and is full of crabs and fish. During a spring tide, the water will go out farther at low tide, and this zone may be exposed to the air for a few hours each day.

SUNLIT ZONE

The uppermost layer of the ocean water is flooded with sunlight—until the Sun goes down, of course. Just like plants on land, the ocean's plants need sunlight to grow. Nearly all of them live in this upper, sunlit zone, which fills the first 650 feet (200 m) of the open ocean. Any deeper and it begins to get a bit too dark for plants to thrive, as the blue water absorbs the Sun's rays. The ocean is much deeper than 650 feet (200 m), and the seabed can be several miles down, so ocean plants do not grow up from the ground as they do on land. Instead they are tiny floating organisms called phytoplankton. Near the surface, there are a million of them in every quart of water, and they provide a food source for all the other animals in the sunlit zone—and for most of the ones deeper down, too.

PLANKTON

Plankton are living things that float in the ocean. They cannot swim well enough to be in control of where they go. Instead, they are carried along by the currents. Phytoplankton are plantlike organisms, also known as algae. Zooplankton are tiny animals that eat the phytoplankton.

This jellyfish uses a bag of gas as a float. The float is shaped like a sail and it catches the wind to drive the fish-eating creature along. Tentacles—sometimes 100 feet (30 m) long—hang down into the water and fire poisonous stingers into anything that touches them.

Portuguese man o' war

Sailfish

This fish is the fastest swimmer in the sea with a top speed of 68 miles (110 km) an hour. It uses its speed to power into a shoal of fish, slashing its spiked snout from side to side to kill prey. It flaps the sail-like fin on its back to herd the fish into a tighter ball, which makes them easier to catch.

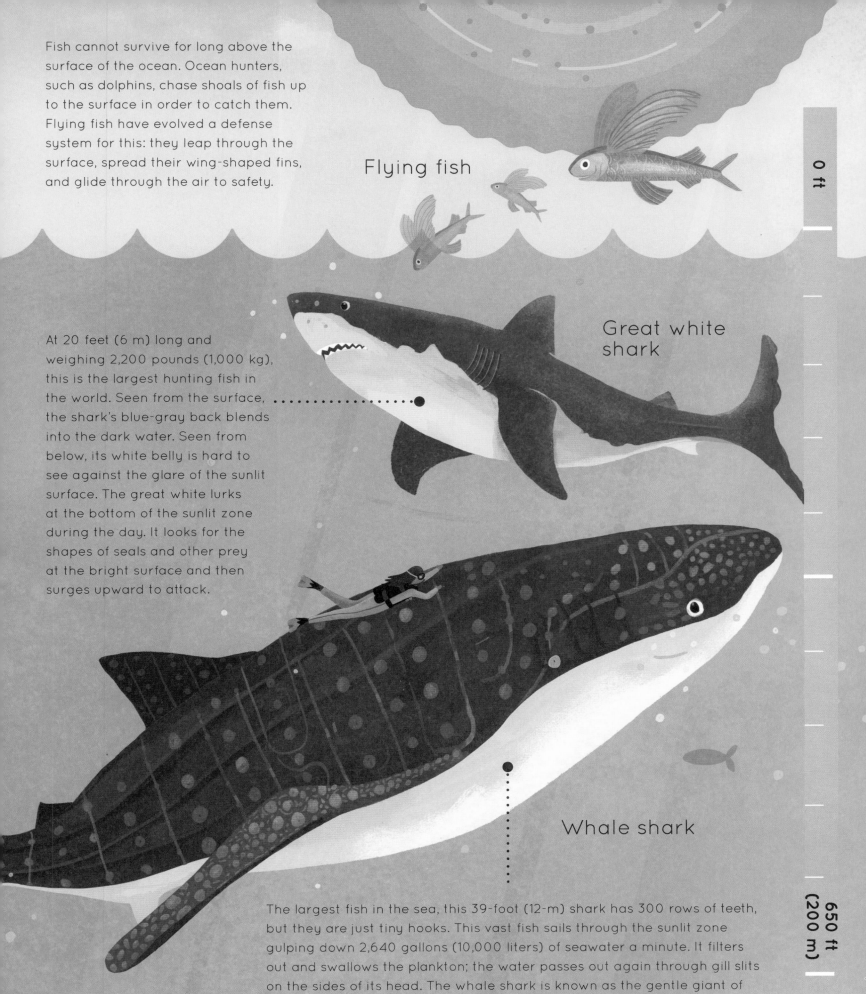

Fish cannot survive for long above the surface of the ocean. Ocean hunters, such as dolphins, chase shoals of fish up to the surface in order to catch them. Flying fish have evolved a defense system for this: they leap through the surface, spread their wing-shaped fins, and glide through the air to safety.

Flying fish

Great white shark

At 20 feet (6 m) long and weighing 2,200 pounds (1,000 kg), this is the largest hunting fish in the world. Seen from the surface, the shark's blue-gray back blends into the dark water. Seen from below, its white belly is hard to see against the glare of the sunlit surface. The great white lurks at the bottom of the sunlit zone during the day. It looks for the shapes of seals and other prey at the bright surface and then surges upward to attack.

Whale shark

The largest fish in the sea, this 39-foot (12-m) shark has 300 rows of teeth, but they are just tiny hooks. This vast fish sails through the sunlit zone gulping down 2,640 gallons (10,000 liters) of seawater a minute. It filters out and swallows the plankton; the water passes out again through gill slits on the sides of its head. The whale shark is known as the gentle giant of the shark family.

0 ft

650 ft
(200 m)

TWILIGHT ZONE

At bout 650 feet (200 m) below the surface, the light from the Sun begins to fade away. Even in the middle of a bright sunny day, it is always an eerie twilight world down here. Going deeper, it is soon too dark for seaweeds and phytoplankton to survive using photosynthesis. The twilight zone is home only to animals, which survive by eating other animals. The smallest, such as comb jellyfish, sift food particles from the water. Many twilight zone animals make their own light, through a process called bioluminescence. This works by mixing chemicals together inside special light organs, or photophores, on the body. Bioluminescent animals send messages using colors and flashes to help them attract a mate or keep a shoal together for safety. Others use their lights to lure prey close enough to gobble them up!

These little fish live in large groups called shoals. During the day they stay deep, out of sight, but when the Sun sets, they go up nearer to the surface to feed. The fish are named after their many photophores, which cover the body. They use them for camouflage by making their bodies glow blue in the surrounding water—so the fish disappears!

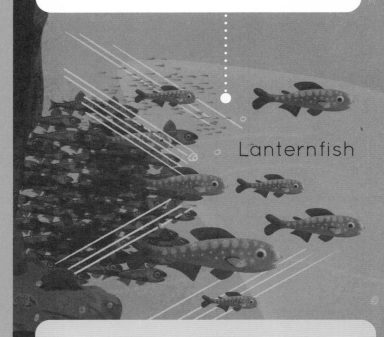

Lanternfish

COOKIECUTTER SHARK

Don't be fooled by this little shark. It may be only as long as your arm, but it gives a terrible bite. Its small circular jaws (with 450 sharp teeth) lock onto the skin of a large victim—a whale, dolphin, or big fish—and then the shark twists its body until it cuts out a neat chunk of flesh. The cookiecutter lives in deep warm oceans and has a long journey to work. By day, it stays right at the bottom of the twilight zone, and then swims all the way up to the edge of the sunlit zone to find food at night, before heading home at dawn.

The barreleye has huge eyes that point upward most of the time, right through the top of its see-through head! This helps it spot the silhouettes of animals moving above against the faint light coming down from the surface.

Barreleye fish

Eyes

This monster of a shark never comes near the surface and it was only discovered in 1976. Although it has thousands of teeth, they are all tiny. Instead, the megamouth glides along, with its big mouth wide open. Its lips glow to attract tiny animals and it sieves out food from mouthfuls of water, using the gills on the side of its head as filters.

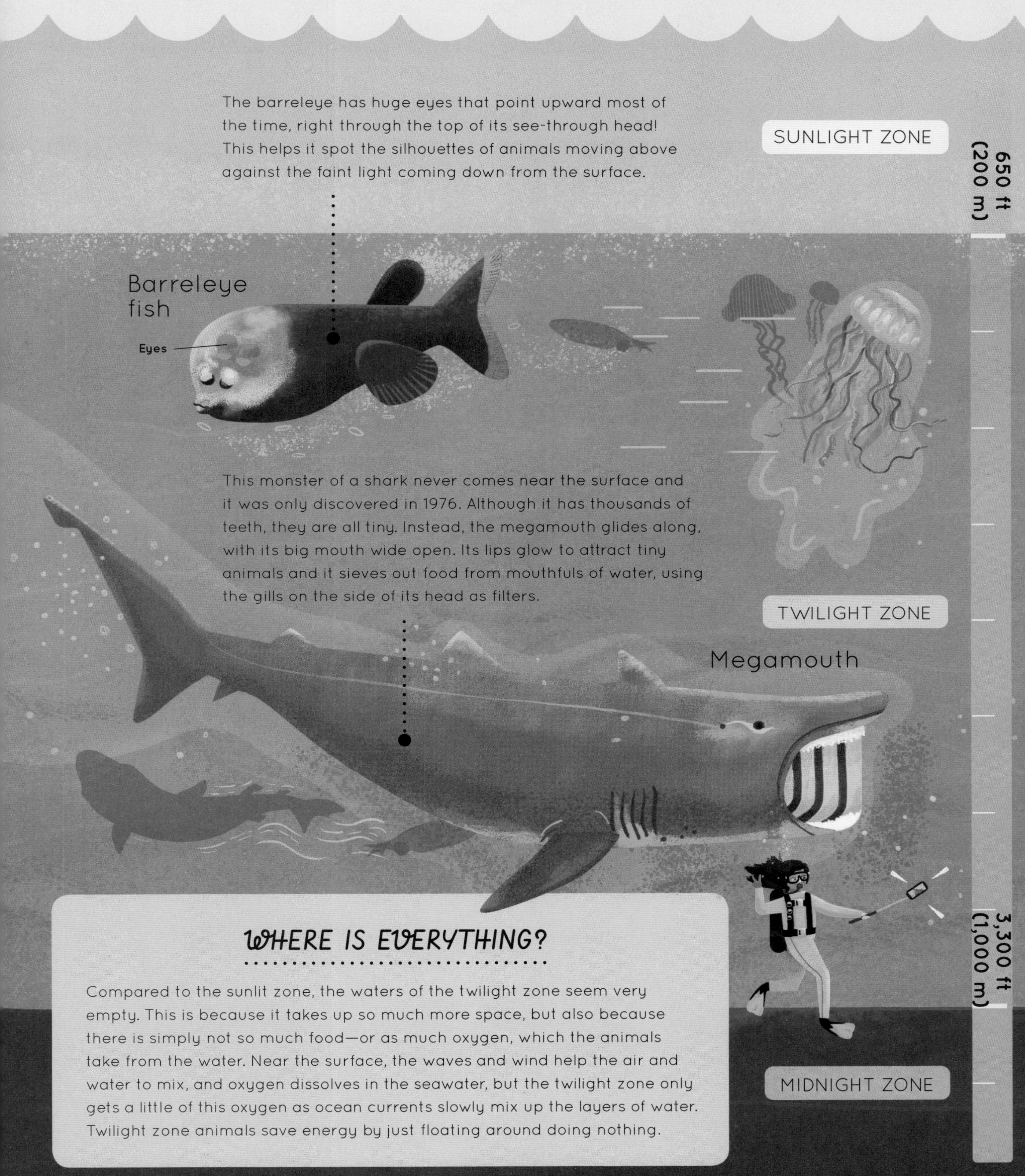

TWILIGHT ZONE

Megamouth

WHERE IS EVERYTHING?

Compared to the sunlit zone, the waters of the twilight zone seem very empty. This is because it takes up so much more space, but also because there is simply not so much food—or as much oxygen, which the animals take from the water. Near the surface, the waves and wind help the air and water to mix, and oxygen dissolves in the seawater, but the twilight zone only gets a little of this oxygen as ocean currents slowly mix up the layers of water. Twilight zone animals save energy by just floating around doing nothing.

3,300 ft (1,000 m)

MIDNIGHT ZONE

MIDNIGHT ZONE

Below 3,300 feet (1,000 m), the ocean becomes pitch black, darker than any night on land. No light from the Sun ever reaches beyond this depth. Things do not change much at this depth. In different oceans and different times of the year, the temperature at the surface can vary widely from being less than 32°F (0°C) in the Arctic to more than 77°F (25°C) in the mid-Atlantic. But down in the dark depths it is always 39°F (4°C). This is the temperature at which water is heaviest, so it sinks to the bottom. The midnight zone is largely empty. There are no plants, and sea creatures are few and far between. It is hard for them to find food.

WATER PRESSURE

Pressure is a force that pushes down on a surface. The air is pushing down on us all the time, but we just do not notice it. Just 33 feet (10 m) of water creates a pressure the same as the whole atmosphere, so in the midnight zone, the water pressure is hundreds of times stronger than at the surface—enough to squash a human and even crush most submarines. The animals down here survive by having soft bodies, where the pressure inside pushing out is the same as the pressure outside pushing in. When they are pulled to the surface, deep-sea fish get all out of shape, like this poor blobfish.

GULPER EEL

In the midnight zone, animals need to be ready to eat whatever they can find. This strange fish is nearly all mouth. Its throat and stomach are so stretchy that the animal can swallow prey that is even bigger than its own body!

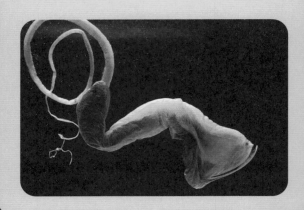

GIANT SQUID AND SPERM WHALES

The midnight zone is where two of the world's biggest animals meet to fight to the death. Sperm whales are the largest hunting animals. They dive into the dark, holding their breath for 90 minutes, to find a giant squid to eat. At 43 feet (13 m) long, the squid are slightly longer than the whale but much lighter. The whale grabs the squid in its long clasp-like jaw, and the squid fights back using a sharp beak and clawed suckers on its arms. At least that is what we think —no one has ever seen a whale versus squid battle in action.

Anglerfish

This deep-sea fish, also called a monkfish, has a glowing lure on the end of a flexible pole that sticks out of its face like a fishing rod. The lure attracts smaller sea creatures (this hunter varies from about 1 inch (2.5 cm) long to more than 39 inches (1 m)) and the anglerfish snaps them up with a single gulp of its toothy jaws.

VAMPIRE SQUID

The scientific name for this deep-sea monster translates into English as "the vampire squid from hell" (although it is actually a type of octopus). The vampire squid uses a disappearing trick to confuse predators. The outside of its body is covered in flashing lights, but the underside of its skirt of webbed tentacles is not. When predators are close, the squid folds this skirt inside out to cover its lights. As if by magic, it disappears.

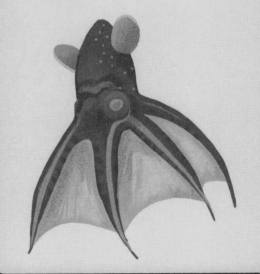

3,300 ft (1,000 m)

13,000 feet (4,000 m)

SEABED

Somewhere down there, below all that water, is the seabed. At deep depths, this can be a hidden world, which is mostly cold and in constant darkness. Few people ever get a chance to go there and take a look. The seabed is home to a range of animals, such as the ones we see near the shore, including starfish and shellfish, and often very different animals, such as giant lice and huge crabs.

There is no seaweed growing out of most of the seabed at great depths. Instead, the seafloor is a vast area of sand and soft mud that builds up in deep layers as bits of grit and specks of dust sink slowly through the water from the surface, creating what is called marine snow. The "snow" is the main source of food for life on the seafloor because it also contains the remains of living things (and their poops!) that have sunk down from the sunlit zone.

JAPANESE SPIDER CRAB

This is the largest crab in the world and it lives on the seabed near the coast (at a twilight depth of about 1,300 feet (400 m)). With its legs outstretched, this gangly crab is more than 16.5 feet (5 m) wide. It could step over a double bed in one stride. The giant crab has a pair of huge pincers for picking up food on the seabed.

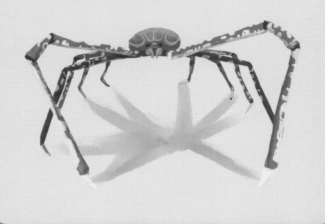

This slimy snake-like fish patrols the seabed looking for the carcasses of large animals, such as whales. The fish has no biting jaws. Instead, its teeth are arranged in spirals, and the hagfish spins its body around to drill into the flesh and suck out a chunk of meat.

Hagfish

An amphipod is similar to a woodlouse that lives on the seabed. However, they can grow much bigger: the largest are more than 12 inches (30.5 cm) long (about as big as a rabbit!). The creature scuttles around the seabed scavenging for bits of dead fish.

Great amphipod

Seafloor fish are often flattened so that they can camouflage themselves among the sand and shingle. There are two kinds of flatfish. The rays are related to sharks, and have an arrow-shaped body and whip-like tail. The others include flounder and sole. They swim upright when young, but then lie flat on one side on the seabed as they get older. As it grows, the flatfish's skull twists, so both its eyes end up looking out of the same side of the body!

Ray

WRECK OF THE TITANIC

Many shipwrecks have been discovered on the seabed. In 1912, the ocean liner Titanic hit an iceberg in the middle of the North Atlantic and sank, with the loss of more than 1,500 people. Once it slipped beneath the water it fell for 2.4 miles (3.8 km), breaking in two before crashing onto the seabed. The wreck was found 73 years later, and has become a haven for seafloor wildlife.

OCEAN TRENCH

The deep seabed is mostly flat and featureless. Mile after mile of nothing except sand and sludge. Ocean scientists call it the abyssal plain—a flat and empty place. However, occasionally the deep seabed drops away into a steep-sided hollow that plunges even deeper below the waves. These are ocean trenches, and the deepest is, as we have seen, the Mariana Trench in the Pacific Ocean. However, there are more than 50 other trenches, most of which are at least 10,000 feet (3,000 m) deeper than the surrounding seabed. An ocean trench has even higher water pressure. The force of the water at the bottom of the Mariana Trench is like having 100 elephants stand on your head (don't try this!). There is even less food than on the seabed. Little is known about the animals that live in this part of the ocean. It is known as the hadal zone, after Hades, the ancient Greek god of the underworld.

Standing for Remotely Operated Vehicle, ROVs do most of the exploring of deep-sea trenches for us. This is much safer, and without a human aboard these small submersibles can explore for longer and go inside caves and other tight spots on the seabed. Usually a ROV is connected to a mothership on the surface by a long cable, which sends back live video of the seafloor. The ROV can also collect samples of mud and animals from the seabed.

ROV

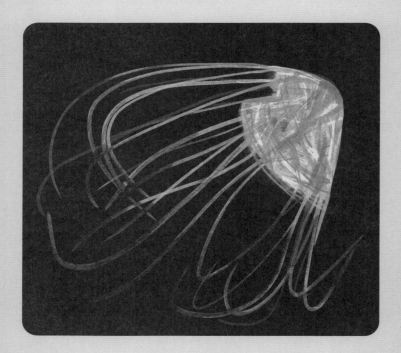

The seabed at the bottom of an ocean trench is covered in a very fine mud called ooze. Most of the particles in ooze are too small to see with the naked eye, but under a microscope they appear as the shell-like skeletons of microbes that have sunk down from higher up, and often formed into beautiful shapes.

Ooze

TRENCH ANIMALS

Fish are quite rare in ocean trenches. Instead, the seabed has shellfish such as mussels that filter the tiny scraps of food from the water. Bristleworms, a cousin of earthworms, burrow into the ooze on the seabed to get at any food mixed into it. Another hadal animal is the sea cucumber, which is a relative of starfish and sea urchins. This tube-shaped creature sifts through the mud for food.

Deep-sea
submersible

The only way to visit an ocean trench is in a submersible. These underwater craft are built to withstand extreme pressure. Unlike a submarine, which can go wherever its crew wants, a submersible has to travel to the dive site aboard a support ship. However, the submersible can dive much deeper than a submarine.

36,000 feet
(11,000 m)

MAPPING THE SEABED

If the water was drained from the oceans, a new landscape would be revealed with mountains, vast plateaux, and deep canyons. Over the centuries, ocean scientists have developed ways to find out how deep the ocean is and what else is down there. Working out what is under thousands of feet of water is not easy, and much of our map of the seabed is blank. But ocean scientists are improving our knowledge all the time, occasionally finding entire submerged mountains.

HMS CHALLENGER

The lowest point on the seabed in the Mariana Trench is called the Challenger Deep because it was measured by the crew of HMS Challenger in 1875. The British ship spent more than four years at sea, recording the depth of the oceans, taking samples of the seabed, and measuring the saltiness and temperature of the water. The information collected during the voyage was used to start a new science called oceanography.

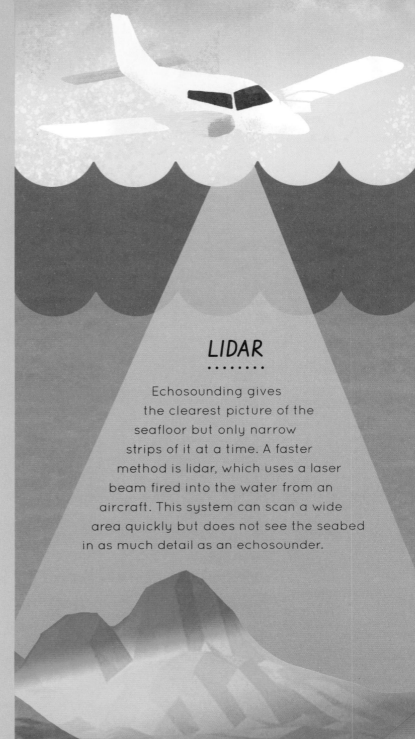

LIDAR

Echosounding gives the clearest picture of the seafloor but only narrow strips of it at a time. A faster method is lidar, which uses a laser beam fired into the water from an aircraft. This system can scan a wide area quickly but does not see the seabed in as much detail as an echosounder.

FATHOMS

The traditional measure of depth is the fathom, which is based on the distance between a man's two hands when his arms are outstretched. That was set at 72 inches (183 cm). The average depth of the ocean is about 2,000 fathoms.

ECHOSOUNDING

The best way of making a map of the seabed is using an echosounder. This is a machine carried aboard—or towed behind—a survey ship. The echosounder sends powerful beams of high-pitched sound into the water. Sound travels well through water, and the sound pulses bounce off the seabed. The sound always travels at the same speed, so the time it takes for a pulse to echo back tells how deep the water is.

BULGES ON THE SURFACE

The seabed is not flat but neither is the surface of the oceans. Scans from satellites show that it has slight bulges and hollows. The differences are small, measuring only inches in most cases. The ocean's sea level is not the same everywhere because Earth is not a perfectly smooth globe. It has lots of bumps and dips, and therefore so does the surface of the ocean.

THE MID-OCEAN RIDGE

The ocean is hiding a very big secret, one that shows us how our oceans and continents are moving, but very slowly. Many millions of years ago, the surface of Earth did not look anything like it does today. The clue is a huge crack down the middle of the seabed called the mid-ocean ridge. While much of the deep seabed is empty and flat, far out from the shore there are volcanic mountains. These form long ridges or mountain ranges, which only rarely poke out of the surface. The middle of these hidden hills is where new seabed is formed. Elsewhere, old seabed is removed by being pulled down into deep ocean trenches, where it melts back into the planet. Let's look at how it works.

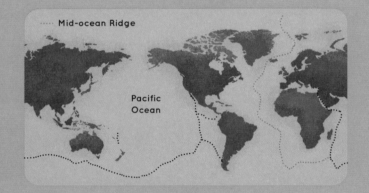

Mid-ocean Ridge

Pacific Ocean

Although no one has ever hiked through it or climbed its peaks, the mid-ocean ridge is the longest mountain range on Earth.

- -

LONGEST RIDGE: 40,400 m (65,000 km)

TOTAL LENGTH OF ALL OCEAN RIDGES: 50,000 m (80,000 km)

AVERAGE DEPTH: 8,530 ft (2,600 m)

AVERAGE HEIGHT OF PEAKS: 6,500 ft (2,000 m)

MID-ATLANTIC RIDGE

The first clue that the oceans had ridges came in the late 1800s when HMS Challenger found that the middle of the Atlantic Ocean was shallower than the seabed on either side. About 80 years later, a survey using an echosounder found a mountain range running down the seabed. This section is called the Mid-Atlantic Ridge. It is over 10,000 miles (16,000 km) long and comes up to the surface at several islands, including Iceland, the Azores, and St. Helena.

Thingvellir National Park, Iceland, lies in a rift valley that marks the crest of the Mid-Atlantic Ridge.

Oceanographers have discovered that ocean ridges are very slowly getting wider. The Mid-Atlantic Ridge is growing by 1 inch (2.5 cm) a year. This happens because the rocks in the middle of the ridge are very thin, and lava from inside Earth rises up through cracks and cools to make fresh seabed. Adding new rock like this pushes the ocean ridge apart, and gradually, the ocean gets wider.

Earth's rocky crust is broken up into large chunks, called plates. Ocean ridges are one place that the plates meet, and where new rock is added. At other plate boundaries, the seabed of one plate rides up over the other, which is then pushed down into Earth, where it melts into lava. This is the process that forms ocean trenches.

Sea floor spreading

Younger crust

Removing old seabed

Older crust

Ocean trench

Seabed

Magma

CONTINENTAL DRIFT

As seabed is made in some places and destroyed in others, the map of the oceans and the coastlines that surround them gradually changes. About 251 million years ago, all of Earth's land was connected into one continent called Pangaea, and it was surrounded by a single ocean called the Panthalassa. Since then, the continents have divided up into the ones we see today. The Atlantic Ocean is still getting wider and the Pacific is beginning to shrink. What will the world look like in another 251 million years?

Permian period
251 million years ago

Triassic period
200 million years ago

Jurassic period
150 million years ago

Cretaceous period
70 million years ago

Present day

HYDROTHERMAL VENTS

Hydrothermal vents are hot volcanic springs on the seabed. They spurt out super-hot water, which mixes with the near-freezing temperatures of the deep sea. The first hydrothermal vents were discovered by explorers in submersibles in the 1970s. They found a strange habitat on the deep seabed filled with animals. Instead of surviving on the scraps of food that sank from the surface, the animals around the vents live on the chemicals released by the hot water.

WATER TEMPERATURES: 867°F (464°C)

WATER PRESSURE: 200 times air pressure

TALLEST: 197 feet (60 m), Poseidon vent, mid-Atlantic Ocean

LARGEST: Lost City Hydrothermal Field, mid-Atlantic Ocean

FIRST DISCOVERED: Galapagos Rift, Pacific Ocean

NUMBER KNOWN: About 185 found so far (estimated total 1,100)

SMOKERS

Some hydrothermal vents are called black or white smokers because the hot water gushes out in dark plumes that look like smoke from a chimney. As it rushes up through rocks under the seabed, the hot water mixes with many chemicals. When it reaches the seafloor, the water cools down very fast and the chemicals turn into a cloud of solid dust and grit.

TUBE WORMS

Hydrothermal vents are home to giant tube worms, which grow to 8 feet (2.4 m) long. The worm's flower-like red plumes collect chemicals from the water and give them to the bacteria that live inside the worm. The bacteria turn these chemicals into food for the worm.

BACTERIA FOOD

The chemicals released by a vent, especially the sulfur coming from black smokers, are used as food for bacteria that live in the water. Similar kinds of bacteria are found deep underground where they survive by eating the chemicals in rocks. The vent bacteria are also able to survive in almost boiling water. Animals living around the vent feed on these bacteria.

ALIEN OCEANS

Biologists have suggested that the microbes living around hydrothermal vents are close relatives of the first life forms to appear on Earth more than 3 billion years ago. They also think that if hydrothermal vents exist on alien worlds, such as Jupiter's moon, Europa and Saturn's moon, Enceladus, then maybe alien bacteria are living there too. These two moons have huge oceans underneath their ice-covered surfaces. The deep ocean of Europa has twice as much water in it than all of Earth's oceans combined!

ANIMAL COMMUNITY

While a vent's water is hot enough to cook an animal, just a few inches away, the water is a pleasant temperature. The number of animals around the vent is 100,000 times higher than in the same area of ordinary seabed elsewhere. The animals range from mussels that filter bacteria from the water to crabs that prey on them—and occasional visitors from the open ocean.

COLD SEEP

A cold seep is a seafloor vent that gives out cold water, not hot. The cold water is often filled with different kinds of chemicals from the hot smokers, including substances similar to gasoline. The cold chemical-rich water is heavier than normal seawater, so it forms a pool on the seabed. This water is often poisonous to sea creatures.

UNDERSEA VOLCANOES

Mountains on land, such as the Himalayas or Rockies, are formed by two plates of crust pushing against each other. One goes under the other and pushes it upward, forming a tall mountain range. On the seabed, mountains form in a different way. Mostly they are volcanoes, where eruptions lay down a new surface of solid rock, which builds up over the years. Oceanographers think that there are more than 1 million undersea volcanoes, although most are now extinct (they no longer erupt). About 75,000 of them rise more than 3,300 feet (1,000 m) above the seabed. Some of them are tall enough to poke out of the surface and form islands such as Hawaii and the Canary Islands. However, most undersea mountains are in deep water, and their summit is far below the surface. These are called seamounts and new ones are created all the time.

HEIGHT: 14,630 ft (4,460 m)

SUMMIT DEPTH: 6,500 ft (1,980 m)

BASE DEPTH: 21,000 ft (6,400 m)

TAMU MASSIF

This undersea mountain halfway between Hawaii and Japan in the northern Pacific is the largest volcano on Earth. The mountain covers 214,000 square miles (553,000 km2), which makes it slightly larger than Spain!

MAUNA KEA

The newest island in the Hawaiian chain is the Big Island. This has several volcanoes on it, with the largest being Mauna Kea. This mighty mountain's summit is 13,800 feet (4,207 m) above sea level, but the base of the mountain is far below at the bottom of the sea. If measured from the seabed, the distance to the top of Mauna Kea is 33,474 feet (10,203 m). That makes the Hawaiian mountain even taller than Mount Everest's 29,029 feet (8,848 m), although nothing like as high above sea level.

During a volcanic eruption, hot liquid rock called lava pours out of a crack in the Earth's crust. When this happens under the ocean, the cold seawater cools the lava into solid rock very quickly. The lava forms a round blob called pillow lava.

Pillow lava

HOTSPOTS

A hotspot is a special kind of undersea volcano that creates a line of islands in the deep ocean known as an island chain. Hawaii was formed in this way (and still is), with its eight main islands and many smaller ones. The volcano is fed by a chamber filled with lava. The lava erupts to make a seamount and then an island that rises out of the sea. However, the seabed is moving very slowly, so the old island shifts out of the way, but the hotspot stays where it is. As a result, when the volcano erupts again, the lava forms a new island. Over millions of years a string of islands is created.

Pumice rafts

When lava is mixed with gas, it cools into a rock that is filled with tiny gas bubbles. This is called pumice, and all the gas trapped inside means that it floats in water. Small chunks rise from the seabed and form a layer of rock, called a raft, on the surface.

OCEAN ISLANDS

An island is a piece of land that is surrounded by water, and the oceans have several million of them. Most islands are just small pieces of rock that poke out of the sea; although about 11,000 are big enough to have people living there. There are two types of island: continental and oceanic. A continental island is separated from its nearby continent because it is surrounded by low-lying areas that have become flooded by the ocean. The biggest islands such as Greenland, Britain, and Borneo are all continental islands. Oceanic islands rise up from the seabed, and are mostly made by volcanoes. Most oceanic islands are small and remote.

GUANO ISLANDS

Many seabirds, such as albatrosses, are such good fliers that they can stay aloft for days at a time and sleep on the wing. However, the birds need dry land to take a rest, lay eggs, and raise chicks. Remote oceanic islands are ideal because most have no land predators, such as rats or cats. As a result, millions of birds visit remote islands each year, and they leave behind many layers of bird poop, which dries into a white substance called guano. Guano is full of valuable chemicals, especially useful as a fertilizer and for making explosives.

The most remote inhabited island in the world is Tristan da Cunha in the south Atlantic. This volcanic island, which is home to about 250 people, is about 1,750 miles (2,816 km) from the nearest city (Cape Town, South Africa).

An atoll is a coral island where dry land surrounds a sea, lake, or lagoon. Atolls exist in warm parts of the ocean, especially the Pacific and Indian oceans. The land is the rock formed by ancient coral reefs that form on top of an extinct seamount. Gradually, the sea washes away the volcano's peak, leaving a flat top just below the water's surface.

HERE BE DRAGONS

The island of Komodo in Indonesia is home to real-life dragons. The Komodo dragon is the world's largest lizard: it grows to about 10 feet (3 m) long from nose to tail. It flicks out its long, forked tongue to taste the air and locate prey, such as wild pigs. The dragon's saliva contains a slow-acting venom, so after giving a nasty bite, the giant reptile simply waits for its prey to die.

BALL'S PYRAMID

This tall pointed rock, off the coast of Australia, is a volcanic stack made from the insides of an ancient volcano. The soft outer rocks have washed away, leaving behind the tougher inner stone. At 1,844 feet (562 m) tall, Ball's Pyramid is the tallest stack in the world, and being only 985 feet (300 m) wide, it is also one of the steepest islands in the world.

CONTINENTAL SHELF

When we look at a map, the most obvious place where the land ends and the ocean begins is the coastline. After all, this is where water begins to cover the land. However, there is another way of looking at it. Earth's land is made up of thick sections of the planet's crust where the rock can be 31 miles (50 km) thick in places. The seabed near the coast is still part of this thick crust and forms a continental shelf, where the water is rarely deeper that 650 feet (200 m). The deep seabed forms a much thinner area of crust that is only about 5 miles (8 km) thick. The thin and thick crust meet at the edge of the continental shelf, where the seabed plunges downward to a great depth. If the water was drained out of the ocean, this shelf edge would be the most obvious boundary on Earth's surface.

When added together, the continental shelves of all the oceans cover an area of 12,448,914 square miles (32,242,540 km2), which is almost twice as big as Russia, the largest country in the world.

ARCTIC OCEAN:
52 percent of seabed is continental shelf

INDIAN OCEAN:
6 percent

ATLANTIC OCEAN:
10 percent

PACIFIC OCEAN:
5 percent

SOUTHERN OCEAN:
13 percent

COASTAL SEAS

Continental shelves extend about 186 miles (300 km) from the shore, and are covered in shallow seas. The water here is crowded with life compared to the deeper ocean. Orcas, seals, dolphins, and sharks are all seen here, and there are forests of long seaweeds called kelp. The giant kelp off the west coast of North America is the fastest growing plant on Earth. It can grow 24 inches (60 cm)in one day!

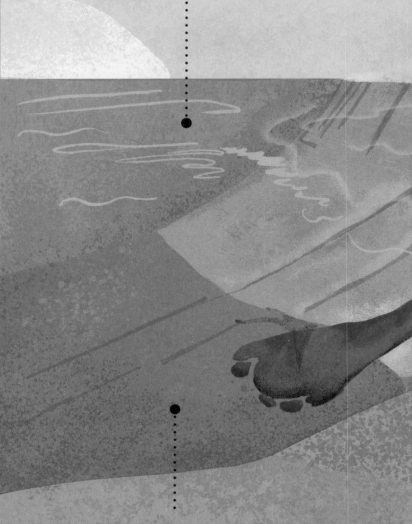

CONTINENTAL RISE

At the bottom of the continental slope, the seabed begins to gradually level out. This section is called the continental rise. The seabed here is covered in mud, sand, and rocks that have washed down the continental slope. A lot of this material used to be part of the continental shelf, but broke off during a storm or perhaps because of an earthquake.

SHELF BREAK

The edge of the continental shelf is known as the shelf break. Here the sea begins to get deeper much more quickly. The seabed forms the continental slope and it keeps going down until it reaches a depth of about 6,500 feet (2,000 m). There are about 186,400 miles (300,000 km) of continental slope on Earth. They can be sheer cliffs that go straight down or be gentle ramps.

SUBMARINE CANYON

The continental shelf is often cut through by an underwater canyon called a submarine canyon. As on land, canyons are eroded by river water, which washes away the seabed to make a V-shaped channel. The biggest submarine canyon is Zhemchug Canyon in the Bering Sea. It is very deep and wide: its volume is 1,390 cubic miles (5,800 km3), which is big enough to fit 100 Mount Everests.

SEA OTTERS

The most famous resident of the kelp forests are sea otters. They survive by diving down to the seabed and collecting a piece of shellfish. They then swim back to the surface and float on their backs: their thick coat of fur helps them float and keep warm. The otter carries a little stone in its armpit, which it uses to smash open the shell to get at the soft meat inside. When it is time to sleep, the otters tie themselves to the kelp so they do not float out to sea, and sometimes they hold hands with each other.

ICEBERGS

Watch out! Iceberg ahead. An iceberg is a chunk of ice that has cracked off the front of a glacier and floated out into the open sea. About 40,000 icebergs make this voyage every year, mostly coming from Antarctica and Greenland. The ice in an iceberg forms on land and then slowly creeps down to the ocean over many years as fresh ice is added inland and older ice breaks off at the coast. The process takes a long time; the ice is around 10,000 years old. The word iceberg means "ice mountain" and often these lumps of ice tower high above the water. The tallest ever recorded was 551 feet (168 m), which is as high as a 55-story building.

WHY ICE FLOATS

Icebergs are not frozen seawater: the water in them is fresh and unsalted. Salty water is denser than freshwater. This means that a bucket of seawater is slightly heavier than the same amount of freshwater. This difference helps the iceberg float on the ocean. However, the way that water expands as it freezes means that a bucket of ice weighs even less than a bucket of water. No other natural liquid does this. Without this unusual water property, icebergs would sink to the bottom of the ocean and large parts of the seabed would be covered in thick layers of ice.

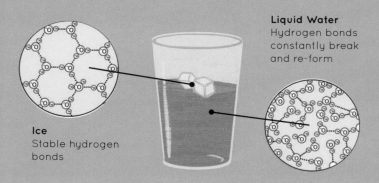

Liquid Water
Hydrogen bonds constantly break and re-form

Ice
Stable hydrogen bonds

It is a well-known fact that 90 percent of an iceberg is under the water. Generally, the iceberg is 30 percent wider under the surface, so ships must not get too close. As they sail into warmer waters, icebergs melt from the bottom up. They can take two or three years to disappear.

DANGER TO SHIPS

Iceberg ice is about one-tenth as hard as concrete. That might sound soft but the average iceberg weighs 165,350 tons (150,000 metric tons). Hitting anything that heavy will severely damage a ship. (The world's biggest ships weigh around 440,925 tons (400,000 metric tons)). Domes and wedge icebergs are also likely to roll over at any time, creating dangerous waves that could swamp a boat that gets too close.

LOOKING FOR ICEBERGS

Icebergs were once a serious danger to ships, especially at night when they were very hard to see—until it was too late. Modern ships are equipped with radar to spot large icebergs, and today satellites scan the oceans for icebergs. Antarctic icebergs larger than 11.8 miles (19 km) are given code names with the year, a number, and a letter A to D. The letter tells sailors in which part of the Southern Ocean the iceberg is.

BERGY BITS AND GROWLERS

Only one in ten icebergs is visible above the surface. Most are small chunks that float just below the water. An iceberg that is less than 16.5 feet (5 m) long is called a bergy bit, whereas one that is 6.5 feet (2 m) or less is a growler.

Tabular: Also called an ice island, these bergs are flat on top and they are at least five times wider than they are tall. The largest icebergs are tabular.

Blocky: Like a tabular iceberg, this has a flat top and sheer sides. However, the height of the sides is much closer to the width, so it looks more like a block than a flat table.

Wedged: One side of this iceberg is taller than the other, and the top slopes down between them.

Dome: This iceberg has a smooth surface but the top is rounded.

Pinnacled: The top surface of this iceberg has at least one steep peak, so it looks like a pyramid or miniature mountain range.

Dry dock: This forms when the central section of the iceberg has melted away to make a gap or channel between two taller sides.

CLIMATE CHANGE AND THE OCEANS

Scientists have found that Earth's climate is changing because of human activities. Many of the changes are having an effect on the oceans by increasing the temperature of the water and making sea levels rise. Climate change is caused by humans adding to the Greenhouse Effect, which is a natural way that Earth stores heat from the Sun. The effect traps heat using "greenhouse gases" in the air. Over the last 200 years, humans have increased the amount of greenhouse gas (mostly carbon dioxide) in the air by burning fuels such as coal and by cutting down forests. This has heated up the planet. The air is now 1.44°F (0.8°C) warmer than 150 years ago, and the oceans are 0.06°F (0.1°C) warmer. That sounds like a tiny increase, but when you add up all the water and air involved, the changes are huge.

WHAT IS CLIMATE?

Climate and weather are not quite the same thing. Weather is the conditions in one place right now, for example cold and wet. Weather forecasters try to work out how the weather will change and warn us if it is going to be very hot or a storm is coming. Climate is a description of the types of weather a place gets throughout a normal year. The climate in the Caribbean Sea is warm and sunny with occasional storms, whereas the climate in the Baltic Sea is almost always cold and rainy. Climate changes could mean these seas get more extreme weather and changes in water temperatures.

Carbon dioxide mixes easily with water. If you add enough, you get fizzy water. The amount of carbon dioxide in the oceans is much lower than this but it is increasing as we add more of the gas to the air. That makes seawater more acidic. Acids are chemicals that react easily with other substances, and an acidic sea washes away rocks faster and makes it harder for animals to make strong shells.

Warming the ocean also changes what chemicals get mixed into the seawater. Normally seawater is mixed with oxygen from the air. We breathe oxygen, and ocean creatures also take it from the water. When water warms up, it holds less oxygen, so there is less for animals to use. Climate change is making it harder for sea creatures to survive.

When you make water warmer, it expands or takes up a larger volume. Heating water by 0.6°F (0.1°C) makes only a tiny change, but even a tiny change across the whole ocean can have a big effect. Oceanographers think that if the ocean keeps getting warmer, the sea level will rise by at least 12 inches (30 cm) in the next 100 years.

GREENHOUSE EFFECT

The Greenhouse Effect is natural. The average temperature on Earth is 57°F (14°C), but if we removed the Greenhouse Effect that would plunge to −0.4°F (−18°C), and most of the land and ocean would freeze over. As its name suggests, the effect works just like a greenhouse, which lets light in through the glass but stops heat from getting out, so the inside is always warm. In the same way, sunlight shines through Earth's air and warms the land and seas. This heat is sent back as invisible infrared rays. However, these rays cannot all shine out through the air back into space. Instead, they are trapped by the greenhouse gas, which keeps Earth warm.

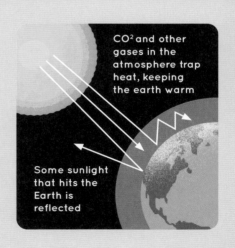

CO_2 and other gases in the atmosphere trap heat, keeping the earth warm

Some sunlight that hits the Earth is reflected

OCEAN WAVES

The surface of the ocean is rarely completely flat. There are normally waves surging across it. Ocean waves are made by wind blowing over calm water. The flow of air rubs against the water, dragging it up into ripples. The ripples catch even more wind and form larger waves. The size of ocean waves depends on three things. Stronger wind makes larger waves and the longer the wind blows, the larger the waves will be. The third factor is the fetch, which is the length of water over which the wind blows. The fetch can be anything from a mile to more than 1,550 miles (2,500 km). Once the wind drops, the waves continue in the same direction as a swell, which will eventually hit land.

SEA STATE

The wave conditions of an area are given a sea state code to help sailors avoid dangerous seas with tall waves. Wave height is the distance from the crest of the wave to the lowest point in the trough behind it.

Sea state code	Wave height
0	0 ft (0 m)
1	0–0.33 ft (0–0.1 m)
2	0.33–1.6 ft (0.1–0.5 m)
3	1.6–4.1 ft (0.5–1.25 m)
4	4.1–8.2 ft (1.25–2.5 m)
5	8.2–13.1 ft (2.5–4 m)
6	13.1–19.7 ft (4–6 m)
7	19.7–29.5 ft (6–9 m)
8	29.5–45.9 ft (9–14 m)
9	Over 45.9 ft (over 14 m)

TYPES OF BREAKER

The shape of a breaking wave depends on the steepness of the shoreline.

Gentle slope: A spilling wave where the crest falls down the front of the wave

Medium slope: A plunging wave where the crest overtakes the lower part

Steep slope: A surging wave where the base travels up the beach ahead of the crest

INSIDE THE WAVE

Although an ocean wave is moving across the surface, the water does not travel with it. Instead the water is swirling in stacks of little circles (or in tubes that run along the wave). As the water circles up, it forms the crest of the wave. The water then moves around and down, creating the trough. In deep water, the wave rises and falls in a repeating rhythm, and the distance between one wave crest and the next (the wavelength) stays the same.

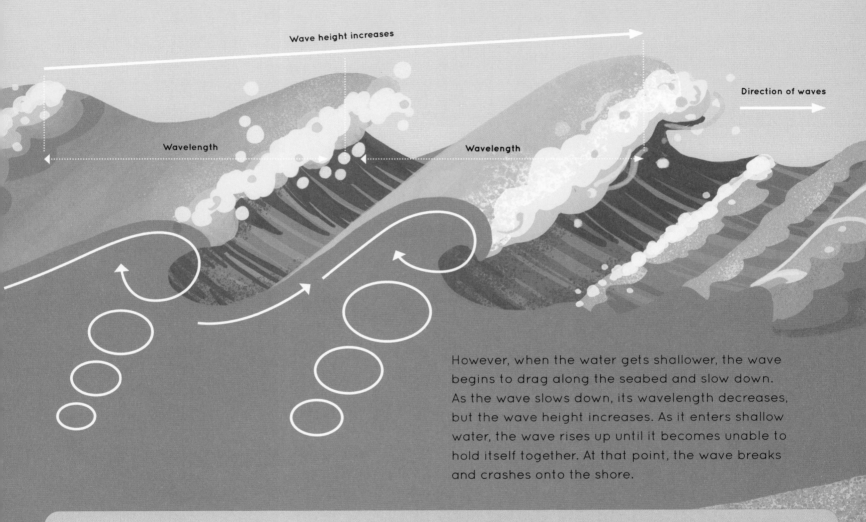

Wave height increases

Direction of waves

Wavelength

Wavelength

However, when the water gets shallower, the wave begins to drag along the seabed and slow down. As the wave slows down, its wavelength decreases, but the wave height increases. As it enters shallow water, the wave rises up until it becomes unable to hold itself together. At that point, the wave breaks and crashes onto the shore.

SEA FOAM

Breaking waves often make sea foam, a yellow-white fluff that collects among the rocks and seaweed. Many people think this substance is from unnatural chemicals, such as soap, that people dump in the ocean. However, sea foam is a natural froth made from the chemicals left in the water by plankton and by rotting plants that wash down rivers into oceans. When they are churned up by the breaking waves, they form a mass of bubbles, like soap in a bath. Even though it is natural, sea foam is not very clean and can occasionally contain poisons made from algae.

TSUNAMIS

The biggest ocean waves are tsunamis. They can be more than 33 feet (10 m) tall and can surge far inland, causing death and destruction. Tsunamis can cross entire oceans in a few hours. They are mainly caused by earthquakes under the seabed, so they are most common around the coasts of the Pacific and Indian Oceans where most of the world's volcanoes and ocean trenches are located. The word "tsunami" comes from the Japanese for "harbor wave." This is because out at sea, the massive wave is often not high enough to notice, but when it nears the coast, it suddenly rises up into a huge wall of water that smashes into the land. Tsunami warning systems pick up the undersea quakes and any shifts in sea height. This means people are normally warned before the waves reach land.

LARGEST TSUNAMI:
Lituya Bay, Alaska, 1958

Lituya Glacier   Landslide

This megatsunami is the largest wave ever recorded, at 1,706 feet (520 m) high. It was caused by an enormous rockslide falling into a narrow bay on the coast of Alaska.

DEADLIEST TSUNAMI:
Indian Ocean, 2004

This tsunami killed 228,000 people in 14 countries onDecember 24, 2004. The wave was caused by a huge earthquake near Sumatra, Indonesia.

KRAKATOA

The loudest noise in recorded history was the eruption of the Krakatoa volcano, west of Java, Indonesia, in 1883. The rumble could be heard in Australia. About 2.4 cubic miles (10 km3) of rock fell into the sea, creating a megatsunami 151 feet (46 m) high, which spread across the ocean. Even the tides in the English Channel were affected by the wave.

The earthquake moves the seabed up (or down) and that pushes on the water around it, causing a wave to form and spread out in all directions. The Indian Ocean tsunami of 2004 was caused by a crack 1,000 miles (1,600 km) long forming on the seabed and pushing or surging up water 49 feet (15 m) in a few seconds.

High-speed surge

The wave is moving at 500 miles (800 km) an hour, but a passing ship would barely notice it. It is only about 39 inches (1 m) high at the crest but has a wavelength of 125 miles (200 km) (an ordinary wave is 330 feet (100 m) from crest to crest). A wave this long holds a vast amount of water, and the sea level drops at the coast as water is pulled out to sea to fill the wave.

Moving
water

Hitting land

As it reaches land, the water looms to a great height and floods far up the land. The flooding is worst in river valleys where the water is being funneled between the hills. Generally, two or three waves hit in total, around 20 to 30 minutes apart as the crests of the wave arrive one by one.

TSUNAMI-PROOF HOUSE

There are about two or three tsunamis every year, although they are not usually big and have an impact on only a small patch of coast. People who live on ocean islands are most at risk from the waves, and they have developed a simple way of reducing damage from tsunamis: they build their houses on stilts, so any high waves just flow underneath!

HURRICANES

Hurricanes are vast weather systems that form over warm parts of the ocean, forming an immense swirling cloud that can be 1,240 miles (2,000 km) wide. The storms that hit the Americas are called hurricanes, but in east Asia they are known as typhoons. Those that form in the Indian Ocean and around Australia are called tropical cyclones. To qualify as a hurricane, the winds inside the storm must be least 74 miles (120 km) an hour. Below that, it is downgraded to a tropical storm. However, hurricanes can grow to be much more violent. The worst kind, a Category 5, has winds above 157 miles (252 km) an hour. If these storms hit the coast, they can cause serious damage. As well as the strong winds battering towns and floods from intense rain, the biggest danger is from the storm surge, where the hurricane pushes a deadly tsunami-like wave far inland.

Weather forecasters watch for tropical storms developing out in the ocean and monitor them to see if they grow into hurricanes. Hurricanes mostly appear during a summer storm season, where the ocean water is warm enough for the weather system to form. At the start of the season, the first storm is given a name starting with A, the next is B, and so on. It is rare that they ever get to Z in one year.

While the eye of the storm is calm and dry, the rings of clouds around it are blown by violent winds. Cold, dry air from the top of the storm blasts down to the sea, while warm, wet air from the surface rises making bands of heavy rainclouds.

High winds

The strongest winds are in the eye wall, the circular bank of cloud that forms the middle of the spiral-shaped storm. This is where the warm air from the surface of the ocean spirals upward. It cools down as it rises, passing its heat to the storm. The cold air creates strong winds at the top of the storm. From above, the storm plunges into the eye, forcing more warm air to rise up and feeding the storm.

THE FIRST HURRICANE

A year after discovering America in 1492, Christopher Columbus sailed back to the Caribbean. The Caribbean Sea has more hurricanes than anywhere else in the world, and Columbus was the first European to experience one. He was forced to sail to the nearest island to sit out the storm. The word "hurricane" comes from the language of the Taino people, who lived in the Caribbean before the Spanish conquerors arrived.

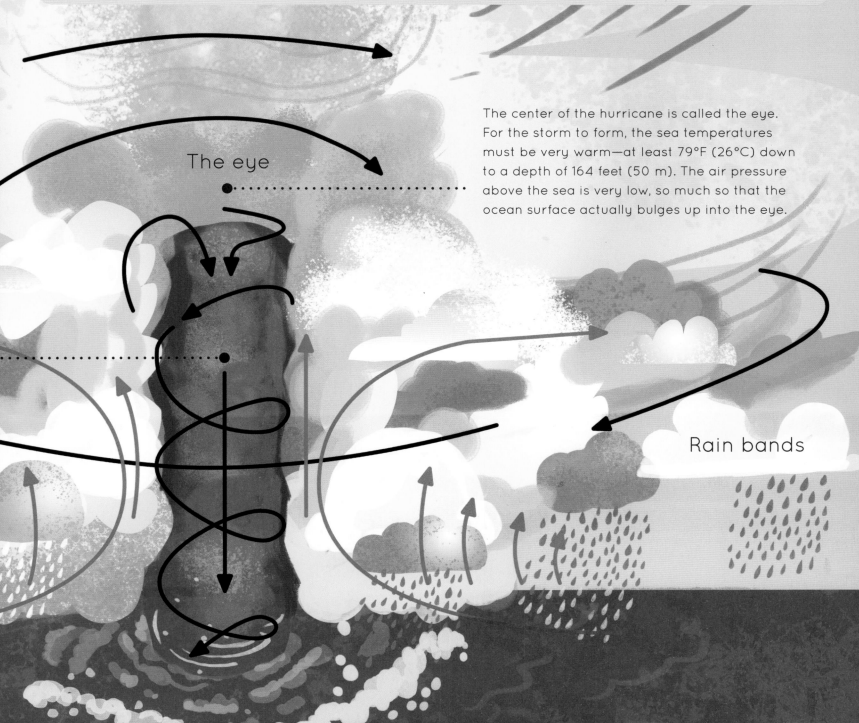

The eye

The center of the hurricane is called the eye. For the storm to form, the sea temperatures must be very warm—at least 79°F (26°C) down to a depth of 164 feet (50 m). The air pressure above the sea is very low, so much so that the ocean surface actually bulges up into the eye.

Rain bands

OCEAN CURRENTS

The ocean is never still: its waters are constantly mixed and churned together by a series of currents. This was made very clear in 1992 when a cargo container fell into the sea during a storm and released 28,000 bath toys—mostly rubber ducks, turtles, and frogs—into the North Pacific Ocean. Over the next 20 years, these toys were carried by the currents. Most washed ashore all around the Pacific from Alaska to Australia and even Chile. Some found their way into the Arctic Ocean and then the Atlantic, with some reaching Ireland after 15 years at sea! This accident was helpful in showing oceanographers how currents work. Today we know that currents that flow toward the equator carry cold water, whereas those that go toward the poles are warmer. This temperature difference is one of the things driving the currents, along with winds and the movement of tides.

MESSAGE IN A BOTTLE

In the days of sailing ships, riding ocean currents could make voyages much faster. In the 1850s, the US Navy began giving ships a free chart of ocean currents if the captain agreed to do more research into currents. Crews were given "drift bottles" to throw into the sea during a voyage. Each bottle had a message inside asking whoever found it to write to the navy, saying where and when it was found. This told oceanographers how the currents moved the bottles and helped make today's map of the ocean's currents.

This current flows from the Gulf of Mexico to the North Atlantic and warms the waters off the coast of Europe. That transfer of heat makes northern Europe's weather much warmer, especially in winter. On the other side of the Atlantic, where cold currents flow down from the Arctic, the winters are much colder.

Atlantic Ocean

Gulf Stream

This cold current running along the coast of South America brings water from the Southern Ocean that is filled with plankton. Vast shoals of fish gather here to feast on this food. Every few years the currents in the central Pacific, including the Peru Stream, change direction. This is part of the El Niño weather system, which causes rainstorms in the Americas and droughts in Australia and Asia.

Peru Stream

Atacama Desert

OCEAN CONVEYOR BELT

The main force pushing ocean currents is a very large loop of water that flows through all the oceans, called the Ocean Conveyor Belt. The main currents move at about walking pace, but the conveyor belt goes slower than a snail. It would take 10,000 years for water to make the whole loop!

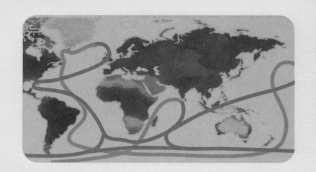

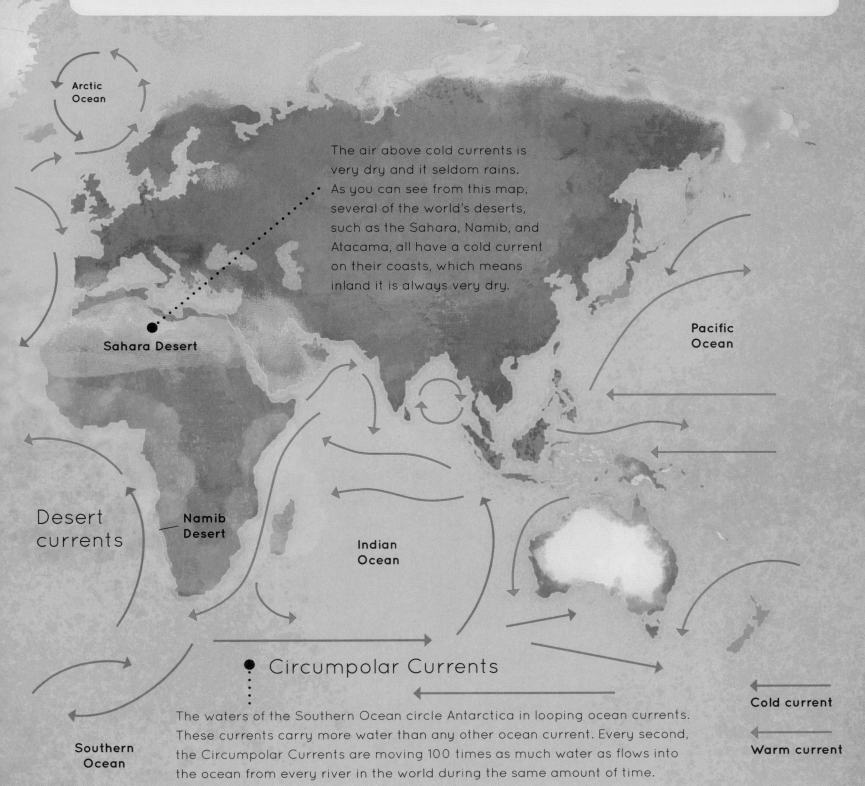

Arctic Ocean

The air above cold currents is very dry and it seldom rains. As you can see from this map, several of the world's deserts, such as the Sahara, Namib, and Atacama, all have a cold current on their coasts, which means inland it is always very dry.

Sahara Desert

Pacific Ocean

Desert currents

Namib Desert

Indian Ocean

Circumpolar Currents

The waters of the Southern Ocean circle Antarctica in looping ocean currents. These currents carry more water than any other ocean current. Every second, the Circumpolar Currents are moving 100 times as much water as flows into the ocean from every river in the world during the same amount of time.

Southern Ocean

Cold current

Warm current

OCEAN FOOD CHAINS

The ocean looks empty, but there is life down there somewhere. Life needs nutrients to survive wherever it lives, but how does this ocean wildlife—all 300,000 species—stay alive in what appears to be nothing but water? To answer that question, we need to trace the ocean's food chains, or what eats what. On land, these connections are easier to see: plants power their bodies with energy from sunshine; plant-eaters such as deer or rabbits consume the plants; predators such as tigers survive by eating animals. The same kind of system is at work in the oceans.

The weight of all the living things in one place is called its biomass. On land, especially in a rainforest or woodland, the biomass of plants is generally about 10 times as much as the biomass of all the animals. Similarly, the animals at the top of the food chain make up much less biomass than the ones lower down. We can imagine this as a biomass pyramid, where lions fill just the point, and the trees and grass make the wide base. In the oceans, this idea is turned on its head. The animals at the top of the food chain, such as whales and sharks, have more biomass than the fish they eat, and the plankton fill just the pointed end of this upside-down pyramid.

Upright Pyramid of biomass in a Terrestrial Ecosystem

Inverted Pyramid of biomass in an Aquatic Ecosystem

OCEAN VIRUSES

The ocean is surprisingly full of viruses. They are less than one-millionth of a yard long. In warm places, there are about 100 billion of them in every quart of seawater! That is about 15 times as many people as there are on Earth! Ocean viruses are similar to the ones that give humans colds and flu. However, the ocean ones are completely harmless to us. Instead, they attack bacteria and other microorganisms in the water, especially phytoplankton. It is estimated that at least one-third of all plankton die from being infected with a virus every day.

Producers

Primary
consumers

Filterers

Predators

Top
predators

Producers
At the bottom of the ocean food chain are the phytoplankton. This tiny plant-like life can only be seen through a microscope. It does not eat food like an animal. Instead, it gathers the energy it needs from sunlight—like a tree or flower on land. This makes phytoplankton a producer, which means it produces the food that all animals in the oceans rely on.

Primary consumers
The next link in the food chain are the zooplankton, which eat the phytoplankton. They are the primary consumers: primary means "first" and "consumer" is another word for "eater." All the other members of the food chain are also consumers.

Filterers
The secondary consumers tend to be animals that sift or filter plankton from the water. These include shellfish, basking sharks, and ocean sunfish. (These are the largest fish with bones. Sharks are larger but have skeletons made from bendy cartilage.)

Predators
The third layer of consumers are predators, which means they actively hunt, target, capture, and kill the animals that they eat.

Top predators
The top predators are those that do not have any predators of their own—or are unlikely to encounter a bigger, tougher killer. The top predators include big sharks like the great white, the polar bear, and the orca. (In a fight, it is generally assumed that the orca would always be the winner!)

CORAL REEFS

A coral reef is like a rainforest under the sea, except perhaps more colorful. Reefs cover just 0.1 percent of the seabed, but they are home to one-quarter of all the creatures that live in the oceans. Most coral reefs are less than 10,000 years old, which is young for the natural world. They grow in water that is somewhere between 73 and 84°F (23 and 29°C) and are never found more than 490 feet (150 m) below the surface. Deeper than that, it gets too dark for corals. Although they might look like underwater plants, corals are, in fact, a relative of the jellyfish. Each coral is a colony of millions of individual creatures called polyps. The polyps have a chalky skeleton around them, and when they die, new polyps grow on top, gradually building rock-like mounds on the seabed, which become home for a whole community of animals.

GREAT BARRIER REEF

The largest coral reef in the world is the Great Barrier Reef that runs down the eastern coast of Australia. It is made up of about 2,900 individual reefs and 900 coral islands, and is more than 1,430 miles (2,300 km) long. The combined reef covers an area of 133,000 square miles (344,400 km2).

Although they are animals, reef corals cannot live in deep dark water. They need the sunshine because they have tiny plant-like helpers living inside them. These algae have a marvelous name: zooxanthellae. They make sugar from the sunlight and share it with their coral hosts. In return, the corals supply the algae with other nutrients and a safe place to live.

CORAL POLYP

A polyp is only a fraction of an inch tall and up close it looks like an upside-down jellyfish. In fact, when young, it floats in the water with its tentacles hanging down like a jellyfish, but when it settles on the reef, it turns over so that its tentacles can sift plankton from the water and funnel it into its mouth. (This is also its anus—corals eat and poop using the same opening!) The polyp grows down into the solid reef and cements itself in place.

Staghorn coral:
These corals grow in branches creating a stony structure that looks like deer antlers or a bush that has lost all its leaves.

CORAL BLEACHING

Corals all over the world are bleaching or going white. The reasons for this are complicated, but it is probably linked to climate change. As the water gets slightly warmer, it also gets more acidic and that change upsets the coral. In response, the coral flushes out the zooxanthellae, and that takes away their amazing colors. Without their little helpers, the corals struggle to survive, and the reef begins to die.

GIANT CLAM

This resident of the coral reefs is the largest shellfish in the world. Its hinged shell is more than 39 inches (1 m) wide and it can weigh more than 440 pounds (200 kg). The clam opens its shell to draw seawater inside and filters out any bits of floating food. Like the corals around it, the clam gets extra help from zooxanthellae living inside.

SEA KRAIT

If you see what looks like a black and white striped eel swimming around a reef, look again. This is actually a snake that dives down and hunts for fish using a deadly venom. Known as the sea krait, it lives in reefs in the Indian and Pacific oceans. It goes to the surface to breathe air and has to slither onto land to lay its eggs out of the water.

Table coral:
Instead of growing upward, this coral grows outward, forming a flat plate.

Brain coral:
These are among the largest corals. They grow into a rocky blob covered in grooves that makes it look like a brain.

Pillar coral:
These can grow to 8 feet (2.5 m) tall, and occasionally branch as they grow so they can also look a bit like an underwater cactus.

PROTECTING OUR OCEANS

The oceans are under attack—from us. Humans have been dumping garbage into the sea for centuries, and we have always just assumed that there was plenty of room for more. However, in the last 50 years, we have started using a lot more plastic, and that never really goes away. Every day, the world adds another 8 million pieces of plastic to the sea, and there are now approximately 5 trillion pieces floating on the surface. They slowly break up and sink to the bottom. Sea creatures cannot tell the difference between plankton and plastic, so on the way down tiny fragments of plastic are gobbled up and enter the food chain. To solve this problem, we are reducing how much plastic we use, and making sure it is not dumped into the ocean. But plastic pollution is just one of the threats against the oceans. Let's take a look at some others.

OCEAN DANGERS IN NUMBERS

 88 PERCENT: The percentage of coral reefs under threat from pollution

 HALF: The number of fish in the ocean compared to 1970

 100,000: The number of sea mammals, such as seals, that are killed by plastic pollution each year

 500: The number of dead zones, where chemical pollution from land kills all life, and covers an area the size of the United Kingdom

OIL SPILLS

As you read this, there are more than 4,000 oil tankers sailing across the oceans. Each one carries enough crude oil to fill at least 100 Olympic-sized swimming pools. Luckily, accidents are rare, but occasionally the oil is spilled into the ocean. The crude oil is useful to us for making fuels and chemicals, but it floats on the water's surface and is mostly poisonous to sea life. It can take several months before the oil spreads out, and even longer if the slick hits the shoreline.

OVERFISHING

Fish is an important food source, and each day more than 4 million fishing boats go out to sea to catch the fish for us. However, fishing technology has gotten so clever—it uses echosounders to find fish—and nets are so large that we are removing fish from the sea more quickly than they can breed. To solve this, each fishing boat is allowed to catch only a small amount of fish each day. Also, long nets often trap the wrong sea life, such as turtles, seals, and sharks, so fishers are changing to use lines and hooks to catch fish.

GLOSSARY

acid
liquid chemical that burns other substances

algae
single-celled relative of plants that lives in water or in damp areas

Antarctica
the ice continent around the South Pole

atmosphere
a layer of gases that surrounds a planet or moon

bacteria
a tiny life form with a body made from just one cell

billion
a thousand million

bioluminescence
a light made by a living thing

biomass
the weight of all the living things

bleaching
a process that turns things white, removing colors

cape
a piece of land that sticks out in the ocean

carnivore
an animal that eats other animals

compressed
squeezed together

equator
an imaginary line that runs around the middle of a planet, star or moon that sits halfway between the north and south pole. The equator divides the object into two halves or hemispheres.

fertiliser
a chemical that is used by a plant to make important chemicals, and which helps it grow faster

gravity
the force that pulls objects to the ground

hemisphere
one half of a globe, such as a planet. Planets can be divided into northern and southern hemispheres or western and eastern hemispheres.

HMS
standing for His or Her Majesty's Ship, these letters are used to name British naval ships

hydrothermal
to do with hot water coming out of the ground or seabed

merchants
people who buy goods in one place, transport them to somewhere else and sell them

microbes
another name for a microorganism, a life form that is too small to see without a microscope. Examples include microbes and bacteria.

millennium
a period of a thousand years

minerals
natural chemicals found in rocks and water

mosoon
a wind system that changes direction half-way through the year. Often that creates a dry period and a rainy period

nuclear reactor
a strongly built chamber where radioactive chemicals are used to generate electricity

oceanographer
a scientist who studies the oceans

organisms
another word for living things

photophores
organs inside an animal's body that makes light

plankton
microscopic animals and algae that float in the oceans

pole
the top or bottom point of a planet, star, or moon

polyp
a jellyfish-type animal that clings to the seabed and points its tentacles upwards. Coral and sea anemones are examples of polyps.

predators
animals that hunt for other animals to eat

pressure
a way of measuring the force pushing on a surface

temperature
a measure of how much heat is in a substance

transparent
another word for see-through

trillion
a million millions

volcano
a hole in Earth's crust through which hot, liquid rock (magma) can leak out onto the surface. Often volcanoes form into tall mountains.

INDEX